# God Gave Me Some Bad Advice

# God Gave Me Some Bad Advice

## Byron Harmon

A Bolden Book

AGATE

CHICAGO

Printed in Canada.

A Bolden Book. Bolden is an imprint of Agate Publishing, Inc.

Library of Congress Cataloging-in-Publication Data

Harmon, Byron.
God gave me some bad advice / Byron Harmon.
    p. cm.
"A Bolden book."
Summary: "A memoir of growing up and surviving tough circumstances in late 20th Century America"--Provided by publisher.
ISBN-13: 978-1-932841-34-3 (pbk.)
ISBN-10: 1-932841-34-2 (pbk.)
1. Harmon, Byron. 2. Authors, American--20th century--Biography. I. Title.

PS3608.A748Z46 2008
 813'.6--dc22
[B]
                        2008009540


10 9 8 7 6 5 4 3 2 1

Bolden and Agate books are available in bulk at discount prices. For more information, go to agatepublishing.com.

*This book is dedicated to:*
*God, whose advice has taken me to untold heights.*

*My family, David, Shirley, Andre, and Marshall Harmon.*
*I am glad that God brought me to you.*

*And the residents of Guinn Street, the Washington Marion*
*High School Class of 1987, and the city of Lake Charles,*
*Louisiana. Without you, I could have never been me.*

# Author's Note

I've always believed that everyone has at least one good story to tell. This is mine. My life isn't more important than anyone else's, but if I can influence one person to put their faith and trust in God, then it's at least worth the ink and paper it's printed on.

Many memoirs are notoriously full of half-truths and holes. Some authors have paid a terrible price for their fabrications and misrepresentations. I want to make it crystal clear that this is a work of memory, not a work of journalism; it is my story, told through the lens of my eyes. This is how I saw it all. The people, places, and events in this book are described to the best of my recollection, and in certain cases I have changed a few names, for reasons that will probably be obvious when you read this book.

THE LAST TIME I SAW MY FATHER ALIVE, HE WAS ABOUT TO DIE. HE WAS at the end of a long and tortuous fight with lung cancer, and we both knew that his time was short. My mother had called and told us that Pops was in bad shape. My brother Andre and I rushed home. We made the hour-and-a-half drive from Baton Rouge to Lake Charles in fifty minutes.

The short walk down the hallway leading to my father's bedroom was the longest of my life. The room was dark except for the weak light from the television showing a generic Western movie. The scent of sickness filled the air and the sight of Pops lying helpless shook me.

*It's not fair*, I thought.

Soldiers are supposed to die on the battlefield, not in their beds. And my father was a soldier, literally. He'd served more than twenty years in the U.S. Army and fought in Vietnam. While I held his skeletal hand, a hand that was once so strong and pulsed with the vigor of life, he gave me advice that only a dying father gives to his son.

"Look after your momma...be a better man than I was...always take responsibility for your actions...trust in God."

His breathing was so heavy and labored that I barely heard him. Lost in a haze of grief and sentimentality, the last words that I heard my father whisper were, "I love you, son."

David Harmon, my late father and greatest influence, once told me the fiercest force on the planet was a *woman*.

It was a warm Saturday morning in the mid-1980s, and we were bass fishing in our little fourteen-foot boat on a local river as a gathering of dark clouds with bad intentions formed on the horizon.

"Son, make no mistake, women are powerful," he grinned, scanning the darkening sky. Pops had a smile that was absolutely fiendish. "That's why they decided to name hurricanes after 'em."

My father, whom I called Pops, loved a good metaphor (never mind that they'd already started using men's names for hurricanes back in '79). It's one of the many traits I inherited from him. Twenty years later, I thought of Pops as I sat in the comfort of my high-rise apartment in Manhattan and watched the dire television weather reports about Hurricane Rita's impending landfall. Rita, it was clear, was some hurricane, angrily churning her way through the Gulf of Mexico. In September of 2005, she let loose wrath as fearsome as a jilted lover's on my hometown, the small port city of Lake Charles, Louisiana. I nervously called my mother, Shirley, and my younger brother, Marshall, who lived with her, but there was no answer. The phone lines into Louisiana were jammed with callers seeking news. By the time I reached my older brother Andre in Baton Rouge, more than a hundred miles to the east, my fingernails had been nibbled down to nubs.

"I don't know where Momma and Marshall are," he said. The concern was evident in his voice. "She left with Aunt Gerry and them." My cousins were caravanning upstate to escape the storm. They were lucky.

With winds of 115 miles an hour and 15-foot storm surges, Rita left wide swaths of Lake Charles under water. All over town, the wooden frames of once-grand homes were scattered like giant toothpicks. Nobody was killed because there was nobody left to die. City officials had sent out the order to evacuate days before the storm hit. Rita was left to swing at plywood-boarded windows, empty streets, and shadows. Nobody was taking any chances—not after seeing what Katrina, that other scorned woman, had just done to New Orleans.

Lake Charles, a heavily French Creole–influenced city of some 70,000 people, is located on Interstate 10 between Houston and New Orleans. The town is also surrounded by water. There is of course Lake Charles, the city's namesake. There is also the brackish Calcasieu River, or Quelqueshue, an Indian term meaning "Crying Eagle." These waterways are connected to the Gulf of Mexico by a deepwater ship channel. Lake Charles is used to water.

Hurricane Rita hit Guinn (pronounced Gwen) Street, the narrow road where I grew up, especially hard. Hundred-year-old trees were ripped from their roots like giant carrots and deposited in the next-door neighbors' yards. Up and down the street the shades and curtains of houses were drawn, but you could still see inside of them—because the windows and walls were blown in. Blue tarps provided by FEMA covered roofs that were stripped of their shingles, and some of the houses still had the dingy watermarks left over from the flooding, looking like the sweat-stained armpits of old dress shirts.

Weeks later, I flew home from Manhattan to survey the damage myself. After ten years of living in the Big Apple as a so-called big time television producer, I felt out of place. I was a stranger in my own neighborhood. Many of the sad and broken people still living there barely recognized me.

It had been nearly twenty years since I "got out" of Lake Charles. As if it were a prison or the Army. A lot had happened in my short life. My father and my grandmother had both passed away, and their deaths had devastated me. Nearly fifteen years later, I still can't bring myself to put flowers on their graves, or even visit my surviving relatives. They think I'm uppity. But honestly, it's too painful to come home.

I worshipped my father and grandmother, Jessie Lee Berry, who was my momma's mother. When I visit my mother, I stare at their pictures hanging on the wall. They raised me and made me who I am. They were the heart and soul of our family, the life and breath of me. Since their passing my insides have been empty as a dry well.

But I was lucky.

Unlike many of my close friends, I successfully avoided the penitentiary, the infirmary, and the mortuary. Too many of them paid a terrible price for staying home. To break out, I had to cheat death by joining the Army. Whenever I went back to Lake Charles, I felt nervous and sad. I'd even check the newspaper obituaries to see who had died recently or been arrested.

All of my old friends are gone, too. I have survivor's syndrome—I constantly ask myself, "What made me so special?" I still remember, clearly, when one of my high school teachers told me that I should have been voted "Most Likely to Fail."

But I succeeded.

I've traveled all over the world, fought for my country, and was awarded combat medals in the first Gulf War. I've won Emmys, one of the highest accolades my industry has to offer. I've published three novels that have been praised (as well as panned) by critics. I have two movie deals in the works. I pay more in taxes than my father earned in salary. I have a gorgeous girlfriend. While my friends could only nap, I've enjoyed the deep sleep of the American dream. Hell, I even lost my accent.

"You don't talk like you're from Louisiana," people from New York used to tell me all the time. As if New Yorkers had any special dexterity with the King's English. Have you ever heard someone from Brooklyn? Now *that's* an accent.

Walking through my wounded neighborhood after Rita, I felt the way I had when I was an American soldier patrolling the bombed-out streets of a foreign country. Even the street sign was blown upside down. I craned my neck to read the dangling words.

Guinn Street was eerily silent. There were none of the sounds that I'd been used to while growing up. No throngs of noisy kids playing in the park across the street. No older ladies gossiping at the fences. No Mr. Sherman working on one of his many old rusted cars. No fathers barbecuing or beer drinking. I daydreamed of a time when that was the soundtrack of my street.

At least the house I grew up in wasn't destroyed. That would have been too much for me. Too many memories were trapped inside that old half brick and half yellow-painted wood ranch-style house. I learned to write poetry in that house by listening to The Isley Brothers and Atlantic Starr on the late night "quiet storm" radio program. I snuck my first kiss (and other things) from fast neighborhood girls in that house. I got caught with marijuana in that house. I caught a lot of ass whippings in that house.

I thought of all of that as I cautiously stepped over tree limbs while closely inspecting the house's outside. The house was intact but the yard was a mess. From years of forced labor in that yard, I knew every foot of its half acre, every blade of grass, every leaf of every branch of every tree. I reached down and picked up a fallen branch that still held the rope from the tire swing that gave me so much delight as a twelve-year-old. Like me, the old tire was long gone and in the wind.

Once inside, I held my breath. The house stank of spoiled milk and rotten meat, but it was still livable. We were lucky. As I looked at the water-soaked tiles hanging from the ceiling in my former bedroom, the once taut and firm house on Guinn Street now sagged in all the wrong places. In that respect, it resembled my life.

# ACT I

## Guinn Street

**T**HE OLDER I BECOME, THE LESS I LIE. I THINK I'M TURNING INTO MY father.

*Like my father?*

That's a concept I used to have trouble grasping, since at an early age I learned that my daddy was no good. At least that's what my mother used to tell me.

"'You're just like yo' damn daddy," I can still hear Shirley Harmon saying. "Keep running dem streets and see where you 'gon end up."

But what my daddy really was, was a hustler. At least that's what the word was on the street. See, my father always had a gun or a knife in his pocket. He was, as they say, a "hard man." He even had a mean way of looking happy (Pops got that from growing up dirt poor, and from his hard-living Army service, I eventually learned). Tall, brown-skinned, and slim, he had the thin face and high-cheekboned look of an Old West gunslinger. In fact, he sort of looked like a black Clint Eastwood, but bald.

My daddy was a Howlin' Wolf blues record come to life. A natural born hell raiser, he went out partying on payday Fridays and wouldn't stagger back home until Sunday afternoon. My daddy gambled, drank too much Schlitz malt liquor beer, and was all too at home in hole-in-the-wall rib spots, pool halls, or "bucket of blood" juke joints. He'd been shot at and stabbed, and on special occasions was willing to crack open a few skulls with a pool stick. But he *always* put food on the table and clothes on our backs.

Like most boys, I wanted to be just like my daddy. While my big brother Andre was close to my mother, I was a daddy's boy. When I was a baby and living on an Army base in Germany, my mother told me that I would cry all day until my father came home. He was the only one who could hold me on the plane ride back to the states.

*Just like yo' damn daddy...*

I guess it was only natural that when *I* came of age, I always had a knife or drugs in *my* pocket. Although I hadn't lived long enough to earn his hard look (I was chubby as a child, not fat, but large enough for my mother to buy me husky-sized clothes from Sears), I did inherit my father's brown skin to go along with the curly hair of my mother.

As a teenager, I gambled, drank malt liquor, skipped school, smoked too much Acapulco Gold, hung out in the projects, and—even though I was just sixteen—spent every weekend in nightclubs, some as far away as Houston, two hours west of Lake Charles. I didn't run with the wrong crowd. I *was* the wrong crowd. I should be dead now.

Guinn Street was the kind of neighborhood where every little boy had a best friend, a bicycle, and most importantly, a father. Most of the fathers were like James Evans from the 1970s sitcom *Good Times*. They were hardworking men who, for discipline's sake, would "cut that butt" with belts or, in the case of one of my best friends, the dreaded extension cord. His screams could be heard up and down the street, and not one parent on the block would interfere. Our teachers and principals were even allowed to whip us at school—and this was in the early 1980s.

They put the *tough* in tough love. I don't care what parenting experts say: There is something to be said for whipping a child's ass. These days, kids are too pampered and soft. You can see the fear in their eyes—real life is just waiting to eat them alive. At the same time, they have no real respect for authority. For my generation, respect started at home.

Our street was divided between the blue-collar chemical plant workers and the lighter-blue-collars of chemical plant engineers, with a few teachers and housewives thrown in for good measure. Up the block was more middle class, as opposed to those of us who were right on the border between middle class and broke-ass. The cars were a little bit newer up the block, the houses were a little more expensive up the block, and the skin tones were a little bit lighter up the block. Little differences like that were a constant source of under-the-surface tension and intra-racial racism in our neighborhood. It was the classic uptown versus downtown scenario.

My parents moved my brother Andre and me to Lake Charles in

1973. My younger brother Marshall was born on July 4, 1976. He was the bicentennial baby, while I'd been born the day man landed on the moon, July 20, 1969. My mother was born on Christmas Eve. Interestingly enough, holidays were never a big deal in my family.

My father had recently retired from the Army after twenty-one years of distinguished service with stints in El Paso, Ft. Polk, Vietnam, and Frankfurt, where I was born. Andre was four years older than me, but we were bosom buddies from birth. The difference in ages between my younger brother Marshall and me prevented us from being as close.

Our house was simple and comfortable, a three-bedroom, two-bath place with large front and back yards. We had just enough furniture to be functional. No frills. My father bought our house for $20,000 from an aging white couple, Mr. and Mrs. Harrington. This was back when Guinn Street still had aging white couples living there. In fact, the whole area used to be lily white. We were just the second black family to move into the neighborhood, and by the time I graduated from baby bottles to solid food, Guinn Street had gone beige. I was too young to understand "white flight." For their part, my parents and the other black parents were too old and broke to care. At the end of the day, all they wanted was a decent place to raise us.

Guinn Street was a great place to grow up.

It seemed that all of the parents on the street must have gotten together and agreed on a mutual time frame for sexual relations, because nearly all of them had kids the same ages. There were at least fifteen boys on my block who were separated in age by two or fewer years. This was a great situation for social interaction, self-esteem building, and bonding for us young black boys. We learned the meaning of unity, but we also were able to define and test our still-forming personalities against each other. And there were always more than enough players for sports and games, which were the center of our young lives on Guinn Street. Oddly enough, there weren't as many girls in our neighborhood, but hell, who needed girls then? Not when there were sports to be played.

Guinn Street had a huge public park nearby, but our main sports arena was the backyard of two of my best friends, Nelson and Craig Joseph. Their family was our neighborhood's version of the *Brady Bunch*. There was Nelson, Craig, and their older brother Morris, all standout athletes. And they had three beautiful sisters, Pam, Jocelyn, and Dedra. Their yard was Madison Square Garden and Texas Stadium rolled into one. On one side of the huge yard stood a sometimes ten-foot, sometimes eight-and-a-half-foot tall basketball goal complete with a concrete court, courtesy of the Joseph's bricklayer father, Sonny J. The rest of the yard was long and wide, perfect for our bone-jarring tackle football games. One sport we never played was baseball, though—too much equipment costing too much money, both of which were always in short supply. Either someone would have a thread-worn old baseball but no bat, or three raggedy-assed gloves and no baseball. But basketballs were cheap and it was on Sonny J's concrete masterpiece that neighborhood legends were made. We played outside year-round, because it was "Africa hot" in Louisiana year-round. The games would begin on Saturday and Sunday afternoons, right after the college and professional teams ended on television. That's when we'd meet up and imitate our heroes like Dr. J., Kareem Abdul-Jabbar, and the entire mid-'70s Pittsburgh Steelers roster. Every game had a soundtrack. Someone would always have a gargantuan radio playing the latest R&B hits at ear-splitting levels. There was nothing like draining a bucket to the sounds of Rick James's "Give It to Me Baby" or "Burn Rubber on Me" by the Gap Band. Our basketball games, sometimes lasting for hours, would always be played with the intensity of Game 7 of the NBA finals.

"You don't want none of this," Nelson used to brag as he dribbled. Only he wasn't bragging.

Nelson Joseph was Michael Jordan before Michael Jordan was Michael Jordan. He even went by the nickname NJ. Two years older than most of us, he was a god in a pair of leather Converse All-Stars. Nelson was tall, around 6'3", with a slim athletic build, and he was always the first person picked, *always*. Didn't matter if it was basketball or marbles, NJ had no weaknesses. He could dunk, run, catch, pass, or shoot with equal ease. He was an authentic statewide sports phenom, always in the sports pages, and lucky for us he lived in our neighborhood. Who gave a damn about Mike? We all wanted to be like Nelson. Many of us wanted to be Craig, Nelson's younger brother. But as we grew up and Nelson's star rose to cosmic heights, we were content merely to be in his orbit. He was our ticket out of the hood. I couldn't wait to become part of his entourage. Oh, how we'd make it rain in the strip club. But Nelson's fame weighed heavily on Craig. Craig was also very good at sports, but it was impossible to compete with Nelson's talents.

We were Lake Charles's version of "Our Gang" or Fat Albert and the Cosby kids. My closest friend on Guinn Street was Matthew Arrington, aka "Miny Mo." We only called him that when we were high—as a kid we used

Dale, his middle name. He lived across the street from me. I met him when we were both just four years old, but Dale was always old for his age. He was quoting Malcolm X in the third grade. By the time he was fourteen, he was six feet tall, slender, and had a full beard with a voice as deep as Barry White's. No one ever, ever, ever believed him when he revealed his real age, most of all the police. Dale was tough, too. While we were playing street ball as youngsters, he was starring at full-contact organized football in just the second grade. He got in a lot of fights, too. One thing about Dale, he didn't argue or give you a long speech before fisticuffs. Just "Pow!"

My other partner and sometimes "play cousin" was Little Harold. His real name was Harold Guillory, but he was short, hence the "little" prefix. The girls called him Handsome Harold. And he was. Well, except for the small squiggly scar from when I accidentally rode my BMX bicycle across his forehead. But scar notwithstanding, Little Harold had a citywide lock on all the hot girls under five feet tall.

We had plenty of other friends, too, like Kevin Hardy. His family was light-skinned and had two cars, so they were considered rich. Kevin lived on the uptown side of Guinn Street and was the comedian of the block—when he wasn't on dialysis. But he was a trooper—his kidney problems never prevented him being a part of our activities. Some summers Kevin was fat, other summers he was skinny. We never treated him any differently than we treated each other. He was the butt of just as many jokes as the rest of us, and he loved it.

There was Obie Davis, who was 6'5" at birth and a dude no one even thought of offending. So I won't now.

A few houses down from mine down lived "Scary Steve" Blaney. He stood 6'2" and weighed all of 115 pounds, and I don't believe he came outside until he was twelve.

Clumsy Chris Archinaud was a jack of all sports but master of none. I can still feel his fouls.

LaRon Malbreaux was a natural-born entertainer. He was short, dark-skinned, tougher than a two-dollar steak, and never met a stunt he wouldn't attempt.

"Hey, LaRon," someone asked at the park after school one day. "I bet you can't jump your bike across that ditch."

"That ditch," which was at least twenty feet deep and fifteen feet wide, was really a drainage canal separating the park from the raggedy next-over subdivision.

"I bet I can," he replied, his extra-white teeth glistening.

In an instant, LaRon became "Dead Man Riding." After constructing a makeshift ramp out of scrap plywood and an old oil drum, he slowly rode his 20-inch Huffy—complete with spokes glittering with multicolored reflectors, and streamers hanging from handlebars—about fifty yards down the street in the opposite direction of the ramp. He waved at the growing crowd and popped a wheelie, "walking" his bike for the last ten yards.

"Evel Knievel can kiss my black ass," he boasted.

After a countdown, LaRon was off, peddling that Huffy like the cops were chasing him.

"Faster," we chanted.

"You can do it," the crowd cheered.

"That negro crazy," a lone voice surmised.

The wind was pure homicide on LaRon's Jheri-curl. He had to be going at least twenty miles an hour when he reached the ramp. More like *crashed* into the ramp. It seems that someone neglected to secure the base of the oil drum. So when the bike rolled onto the ramp, the ramp rolled away—sending LaRon, whose hands were firmly secured to the Huffy's handlebars, headfirst into the canal. The last thing we saw was his Jheri-curl flying behind him like a long, greasy cape.

Seconds later we slowly crowded around the canal, not sure of what we'd find. At the bottom lay LaRon, twisted up like an advanced yoga instructor.

"Evel Knievel...can kiss my...black ass," he groaned.

The whole neighborhood was full of colorful characters. Like the shadowy Al Dino, an unlicensed neighborhood street pharmacist. Al Dino wore a monstrous Afro with a black-power-fist pick positioned in it at the perfect geometric angle. He was so cool that he was frozen. We'd never see him coming. He'd just materialize on the scene out of the ether. He walked and spoke in slow motion.

"Holla'...at...me...you...know...you...want...to," he'd drawl.

His legend was set in stone when word filtered back to the hood about one of his many court appearances. Appearing in front of a judge on charges of jaywalking, Al Dino pleaded insanity. Case dismissed. We didn't know it at the time, but the source of his coolness was a potent flow of opiates that would have made the Grateful Dead proud.

And then there were the dreaded Browns. While not technically residents of Guinn Street (they lived one block over on Medora Street), their shadows darkened our corners. They were always coming from or going to a funeral or court proceedings. Well known in law enforcement circles, the Brown family was like the plague, wreaking holy terror on nearly all who came in contact with them. They were similar to the Corleones, only handicapped. Seriously—they had names like "Crip," who was of course slightly crippled and wore one regular shoe on his right foot and a gigantic Frankenstein boot and iron brace on his left one. Crip had a brother nicknamed "Captain Crunchy," whose face and hands were hideously burned when his cousin, "Dastardly," set his bed on fire one night. Or maybe his brother "Trouble T-Roy" was the arsonist.

The neighborhood was in genuine fear of this family. It seemed at least twenty people lived in their small green shotgun house. Correction—at least nineteen of them lived there. Their ancient white-haired grandfather, a dead ringer for Uncle Ben, lived on a disgusting loveseat on the front porch. He never left that couch. I think they buried him with that couch. All of the Browns had been to jail, even the grandmother. I still get scared thinking about them, especially on cold, unforgiving dark nights when the moon is full and the wind is whistling. However, I don't fear any retribution upon publication of this book, for I am certain that none of them can read.

But the Browns notwithstanding, Guinn Street was still the kind of place where your eight-year-old could leave the house in the morning and come back at night without getting molested. It was the kind of place where the lady who sold frozen Kool-Aid cups wasn't also a serial killer. It was the kind of place where parents and schoolteachers were free to beat the hell out of children and never once have to worry about getting a visit from the state. It was the kind of place where the good old days were yesterday. Guinn Street symbolized a simpler time. A time before crack.

**A**S A KID, I NEVER HAD A NEED FOR AN ALARM CLOCK. I HAD POPS. "Get your ass up!" he'd bark, banging his fist on my bedroom door. "It ain't your birthday."

David Harmon didn't play. All spit and polish, he was a retired career U.S. Army officer who ran our household like a drill sergeant. He never treated Andre and me like little boys. No baby talk. No catch in the back yard. It was work, work, and more work. Even when we were very young, he'd speak to and treat us like grown men. It was hard being a kid in our household. Every day, and I mean *every day*, like clockwork, Andre and I would get up just after dawn. After eating and then making our bunk beds to "quarter-bouncing" precision, we'd commence to wash the dishes and dry the dishes or cut the grass and rake the leaves or bag the leaves or clean out the garage and sweep the driveway or wash the car or edge the grass and pull the weeds or wash the clothes or fold the clothes and vacuum the living room.

"Momma need to have some damn girls," I used to say, under my breath of course.

It was all to instill in us a sense of discipline and work ethic. It's lasted a lifetime and has carried over into the way I conduct my daily affairs today. I'm thirty-eight years old, and I still don't sleep in. Not even on my birthday.

My mother's name is Shirley, but most everybody called her Miss Shirley. She came from the small town of Oberlin, Louisiana. The town had a heavy mix of Creole, Native American, and black bloodlines, which combined to create a community with an unusually high percentage of attractive-looking people. My mother was no exception—with her caramel skin and long silky hair, she was a bona fide beauty queen, as were her sisters.

I love my mother more than life itself, but back in the day she wasn't exactly what you'd call warm. Oh, later on, once we were living on our own dime, Miss Shirley became the June Cleaver of Guinn Street, but when we were young, she was more like Mommie Dearest. Getting her to buy me a simple treat from the store was like a slave asking his master for freedom. The answer was always the same:

"Momma, can you buy me a bag of marbles?"

"No. I ain't got no money for no damn marbles," she'd snap.

"Momma, can you buy me a pack of Now and Laters?"

"No. I ain't got no money for no damn Now and Laters."

"What about..?"

"*Hell* no."

"How 'bout…?"

"Boy," she'd warn, staring daggers at me. "Don't make me buy a belt out this store and beat yo' ass."

*How could she have money to buy a belt but not marbles?* My young mind would wonder.

It was just plain embarrassing. Our house was the only one in the neighborhood where other kids never visited. It might as well have been haunted. During the holidays, no Christmas lights illuminated the outside of our house, no flags on the Fourth of July; on Halloween, there was no candy for the trick-or-treating local kids. It didn't help that we always had mean dogs as pets, like bloodthirsty pit bulls and vicious German shepherds. We rarely had any company. My mother and father didn't play that.

"I don't want them lil' Negroes in my house," Miss Shirley would say.

Until I was in the ninth grade, I had to go to sleep at 9 pm every night. We even had bed check. Oh, and the phone had *better not* ring after 6 pm. If it did, and it was for Andre or me, we'd get clowned.

"Hey, what's popping, Charmagne?" I'd purr. But before she'd have a chance to answer, Pop's voice would boom on the line.

"Byron? What the hell did I tell you about phone calls after six?"

Click. Goodbye, Charmagne, and any hint of a pubescent love life.

I was bitter about my parents' strictness. I can laugh about it now, but back then I actively plotted their assassination. Once I became older and realized that most of my friends were either dead, strung out on drugs, or in jail, I understood that my folks were just protecting us from a *cold* world.

But back then I wanted to be *cool.*

Besides, they were country folks, and we had it *way* better than they did. And they never let us forget it.

"Boy, when I was your age," Pops would say, "I had to walk ten miles to school."

Pops also had a wry way of molding the truth to fit the situation. Hear him tell it, he ran away from the tiny lumber town of Hickory Flat, Louisiana when he was twelve and supervised grown men on the railroad before joining the Army at fourteen. He was the king of sob stories. But my mother could always trump him when it came to tragic childhood experiences. Take holidays for instance:

"You better be happy," she warned one Christmas after I had opened my present expecting to see a Rock'em Sock'em Robot game but instead was left staring at a pair of flannel pajamas that were a size too small. "When I was your age, all I got was a sack of oranges for Christmas."

My mother's background was backwoods. Oberlin was a rural town sharply divided along racial lines. You had four main groups of people: regular white folks, Creoles, cracker-ass crackers, and black folks. I spent all of my early summers in Oberlin, oftentimes working alongside my Grandmother Jessie Lee, who was a cook at Lucy's Café. Incredibly, Lucy's was segregated as late as 1978. There are still small backwater towns in Louisiana that are segregated. My grandmother, who looked like Lena Horne to me, was extremely light skinned and the only person of color allowed on the white side of Lucy's Cafe. To *serve*, that is. For my grandmother's part, she couldn't stand white people, either.

I was, of course, very naive about race relations myself. For the longest time I actually thought my grandmother Jessie Lee was white. Those summers working at Lucy's Café had a profound effect on me. Even growing up in the 70s and 80s, the Louisiana I lived in was a very segregated place. I never had any regular interaction with white people until I joined the Army. I couldn't tell the difference between a Jew, Italian, or Irishman. All white people were, well, just white people. My whole world consisted of being around black people, except for a few schoolteachers and cops.

Our ancestral records were sketchy. On my father's side, the family historian was his mother. Her name was Lee. We called her Mo' Lee. Mo' was a corruption of the term "grandmo'"—itself a corruption of the term "grandmother." Born near the beginning of the twentieth century, all she could tell me was that her great-grandmother was a slave. My daddy's daddy died before I was born. I can only recall one photo of him, an old dusty black and white picture that gave me nightmares. He was one tough-looking man. I can tell you this much—they don't make men anymore who looked like my grandfather looked. You can only acquire that hard stare if you were a black man born in the early 1900s and dealt with the things a black man had to deal with in the early 1900s. My father used to joke that back then you could shoot, stab, or beat a black man but that you still couldn't kill him: "These days a nigga will go to the emergency room if they get a cold."

Mo' Lee lived on a genuine farm with horses, cows, and plowed fields. I didn't spend too much time at Mo' Lee's farm because honestly, she would put our asses to work.

I spent the bulk of my summer vacation at my grandmother Jessie's, who had a more relaxed attitude toward my leisure. Her people were French-Creole-Irish. Her grandfather was named Jim, and she described him as "a one-legged Irishman." Grandma Jessie spoke Creole, a patois type of French, and had siblings with names like Bijeaux, Bideaux, and Rouge. Everybody on Grandma Jessie's side of the family looked like white people. We got "coloring" from my grandfather. His name was Curtis Brown Sr., but for years I thought his name was "that black mutha..."

Curtis Brown was cut from the mold of Mister (Danny Glover's character from the movie *The Color Purple*.) The stories my mother and aunts told us about him are legendary. Sitting around Grandma Jessie's hot kitchen drinking hot chocolate and eating homemade biscuits, my mother would casually ask one of her sisters, "Joyce, 'member the time Daddy broke my arm and knocked me out with that tree branch?"

"Ahh," the room would cackle in laughter while my mouth hung open in horror.

"Then he made you scratch his ashy-ass back," my other aunt, Aline, would add nonchalantly. It was if they were discussing old football injuries.

Everybody had a story about Curtis Brown. It always began with "'member the time...?"

"'Member the time he dragged you out the movies by yo' hair?" my Aunt Jerry asked.

"'Member the time he made James and BooKay (my uncles) take a bath in that washtub outside in the winter?" Joyce joked. "It was twenty degrees. Frost and icicles was hanging off them boys' ass. Huh, momma?"

Mo' Jessie would always remain silent, lost in the smoke curling from her unfiltered Pall Malls. She had stories about my granddaddy that were too terrible to tell. One humid June evening, Curtis Brown had gone out for ice cream and never came back.

My mother has three sisters, Joyce, Aline, and Jerry, whose beauty was renowned in every section of Oberlin, where there are men who are still pissed they couldn't get a date with them as teenagers. Around town they were simply referred to as "them Brown girls." They had two brothers, James and Curtis Brown Jr., but nobody called him Curtis Jr. Since he hated Curtis Sr. the man, I am sure he also hated the name. We called him BooKay (pronounced bouquet, like the floral arrangement), and he fancied himself a professional gentleman of leisure. How my uncle got his nickname has been lost to the ages.

James and BooKay were like night and day. James was conservative, had a loving wife and son, and owned his own business, a thriving fish market in Atlanta. On the flipside, BooKay dressed flashy like a pimp, smoked weed, had a fat bankroll to spend on his many women, and lived in Los Angeles. Guess who was my favorite uncle.

One of my fondest memories from childhood occurred every October. That's when the big fair came to Oberlin. It was a small-town carnival with plenty of cotton candy, grape Nehi sodas, games, and amusement rides like The Scrambler. I used to lie awake at night smiling, whispering to myself, "The fair is coming." BooKay used to drive down from California in his long white Cadillac pulling an ice cream truck. When he'd get to Oberlin, he'd drive all around town blasting Earth Wind and Fire while selling Eskimo pies and empty ice cream cones stuffed with marijuana. He called it "high' scream." BooKay would peel off Andre and me each thirty dollars to spend at the fair, a fortune for a kid in the late 1970s. Uncle James, by contrast, would give us each two dollars.

"I got a damn family to feed," he'd grumble.

I learned so much from my uncles. Their lessons shaped a major part of my philosophy of life. Being around them was like going through boot camp for boys. James taught me how to be tough. He'd had a hard life and he always told me never to expect a handout from anyone. BooKay taught me how to be cool and carefree. He didn't seem to take life too seriously. BooKay was militant. He used to say that he "wouldn't even pick the cotton out of an aspirin bottle." My uncle was the first to expose me to black pride, at least indirectly. After one of his numerous prison stints, he'd converted to Islam. He admitted this one night at the dinner table at my grandmother's, just as she'd finished serving a heaping plate of pork.

"Momma, I don't eat swine any more," he declared. "I'm a Black Muslim."

The table fell silent, shock registered on our faces. Now, you have to understand, in the small town of Oberlin there was only one religion— God. Not Allah, not Jehovah, just good old-fashioned God.

Mo' Jessie sucked her teeth. "Black Muslim, my ass. Boy, I don't want to hear that mess. You better eat these damn pig feet."

I didn't have very many years with my uncles. Like too many of the people who've influenced my life, their lives ended tragically. Early one morning in 1981, Atlanta police officers were called to Uncle James's fish market. As they entered, they stepped over scattered fish and kicked overturned boxes. In a tiny backroom, they found my uncle stabbed to death, the victim of an apparent robbery. James's death was a devastating blow to my family. I still get chills when I think of the way my mother screamed in anguish, and how tenderly my father consoled her. There was a big portrait of Uncle James that hung in the guest bedroom at my grandmother's house. I always thought that painting was so cool—it was like he was royalty or something. After his death, sometimes I'd shut the door and stare at his painting, smiling and crying at the same time. His gruff voice would echo inside my mind.

"I got a damn family to feed."

Five years later, the cops were called to Uncle BooKay's small apartment in Los Angeles. In the bathroom, they found my uncle's naked body sitting upright in a dirty tub full of stagnant water. The death was ruled suspicious. My young world immediately spun out of control. I was too scarred to attend the funeral. To this day, when I see an old-style white ice cream truck and hear its jingle, I think of Uncle BooKay.

Grandmother Jessie Lee taught me a lesson in how to deal with adversity. She was a rock; she didn't shed one tear at her sons' funerals. My grandmother was a hard woman. She had seen too much death and experienced too much pain in her long life to cry.

I never knew if either of my uncles' killers were ever brought to justice. I was just a kid when these things happened to them, and afterwards, my family didn't speak much of the violence that was done to them. But the deaths of my uncles signaled my introduction to violent loss. Summers in Oberlin would never be as carefree.

**M**Y MOTHER NEVER MET A PENNY THAT SHE DIDN'T PINCH. SHE WAS what one would call frugal. There weren't many name-brand items in our house, especially in the cupboard. However, it was impossible not to know what you were looking for since all of our food was clearly labeled, in black and white. No Wonder Bread; the clear plastic bag just read "Bread." No Uncle Ben's—just "Rice" stamped on the side of the small cardboard box. Froot Loops? Please.

We ate rice and gravy every day for dinner. Some days it was rice and gravy with chicken backs and thighs. Other days it was rice and gravy with neck bones. Mostly, it was rice and gravy with a little bit of rice and gravy. But we never went hungry.

On the other hand, my father was a spendthrift—as long as he was spending on something for himself.

"Daddy, can I get an allowance?" I'd ask.

"Your allowance is on that plate."

Up until I was about eight or nine, my father worked full-time at Canalco, a local petrochemical plant, and part-time as a deputy sheriff. Pops believed in working. He was never without a job. But he and my mother always poormouthed about our lack of disposable income. Hear them tell it, we were in the midst of the Great Irish Potato Famine. But for the life of me, I couldn't understand how my father could afford a new Buick, a customized van (with a rollaway bed and icebox), and a tricked-out bass boat. Later on, after witnessing him ease the fears of bill collectors with the finesse of a hypnotist, it was clear how he could afford it. Like our neighbors, he was in debt up to his eyeballs. I was never taught anything about being fiscally responsible. I didn't know the first thing about investing, or protecting my credit score. Later on, when I found out that I had a FICO score of 500, my reply to the loan officer was, "Wow, that high?"

To earn extra money, Pops moonlighted as a pool shark. My daddy was nice with the stick. When I was a teenager, I tagged along with him to neighborhood speakeasies where I once witnessed him running the tables for five straight hours. David Harmon was a sharp dresser, too. He had rows of suits and matching hats, which he called "brims," in his closet. But none of this largesse trickled down to my brother Andre and me.

My parents were particularly indifferent when it came to buying us quality footwear. They just didn't care. They couldn't have. Who else bought their kids sneakers at a grocery store? We'd be in Kroger's buying our monthly allotment of "Rice" and "Gravy" when Shirley would snap, "Go over there and get a pair of tennis's."

"Huh?" I frowned at my mother like she'd just asked me to eat a bowl of dog food.

She impatiently pointed toward a bin holding at least fifty pairs of thick-soled monstrosities, all laced together. They had enough rubber on them to make a set of tires.

"Them ugly cheap things? They're green and orange!"

The grocery basket my mother was pushing screeched to a halt. "And your ass is black," she barked. "But if you don't go over there and get a pair of them damn shoes, it's gon' be black and blue."

It was like a warden asking a man in the electric chair to flip his own switch. Those Kroger shoes set my social calendar back at least a year.

And then there were the baggy pants. During my eighth-grade year, I was elected vice president of the National Honor Society. At the time, I was a very bookish kid—I spent long hours devouring encyclopedias and books on science, religion, and history. I relished knowing things my peers didn't. Oftentimes, I'd show off my obscure knowledge in class.

So I was very cocky when I got elected vice president. It was a huge honor, and it ushered me into the social elite at Ray D. Molo Middle School. The organization's uniform was the official light blue and white National Honor Society T-shirt. It was to be worn *strictly* with straight-legged white pants. The highlight of the school year was the induction ceremony. All of the students attended, along with many dignitaries from across the city. I, as vice president, would be one of the keynote speakers. But I didn't own any white pants.

Now, my mother only bought us new clothes at the beginning of the school year, so I knew this would be dicey. But since this was a big honor, my mother made an exception and promised she'd buy me a pair of white pants. Weeks went by and still no white pants. I dared not inquire. Finally, the day before the ceremony, she came home from work with a bag from a store in the local mall called Chess King. *Thank God the bag isn't from Kroger's,"* I thought. I grabbed the bag and unfurled the pants. I held the pants up to the light. The pants weren't white but off-white. No, not off-white, but damn near tan. Not only that, they weren't even regular straight-legged pants. They were baggies—the kind Morris Day and The Time used to wear. The kind MC Hammer would eventually wear, ten years later. Tears welled up in my eyes.

"Momma, I can't wear these."

Steam poured from Shirley Harmon's ears. "Boy, I paid twelve dollars and ninety-fo' cents for those pants. You're wearing them or you're wearing your drawers."

The next day, the day of what was supposed to be my finest hour, I gave a speech in front of 1,500 people wearing a pair of tan baggies. I looked like Aladdin's genie.

This was neither the first nor the last in a long series of embarrassing moments I'd endure as a kid. I became an expert in the fine black art of "playing it off." Like the time my mother sent me on a class trip to Six Flags in Houston with a grand total of six dollars in my pocket.

"Hey, Byron, wanna play this game?" a classmate would ask.

I'd look at the price and do some quick arithmetic. "Nah," I'd say. "I don't like that game."

"What about that one?"

"Nah."

"How 'bout this?"

"I'm just not really into games."

C'mon, what kid wasn't into games? I guess it could have been worse. My buddy Dale's momma sent him to Six Flags with two dollars.

The Harmon household was not known for setting trends, either. We always seemed to be at least a year or two behind the Joneses. For instance, when other families got Nintendo, we got Atari. When other families bought a VCR, Pops got a great deal on a Betamax. My record player was so old that if it broke down, Thomas Edison would have been the only person who could repair it. Instead of that classic static sound, it produced a noise like a slab of bacon frying in the background. Whenever I'd play Rick James's "Give It to Me Baby," it sounded like he was talking about breakfast.

W HEN IT COMES TO FASHION, MY BROTHER ANDRE HAS ALWAYS been well suited. As a kid, I never saw him get dirty, or even really sweat—probably because he didn't want to mess up his outfit. While I was getting funky playing sports in the park, he was in the mirror. He was, and remains, one of the sharpest dressed dudes I've ever known to come out of Lake Charles, and there were plenty. We had our own legendary local fashion icons, like Kevin Doucet, David Simien, Ernest "Bubba" McCarthy, Kevin Pete, and Darrell Guidry. As young guys we called them Murder Inc., because they dressed to kill.

Our town, small as it was, was still an incubator for cutting-edge styles. Our fashion showcases were the high school football games, the dances, and Sunday nights at the skating rink. Kids would select their outfits with the attention of craftsmen. But Andre was a cut above the rest. Dark and slender, with short curly hair that was always immaculately coiffed, this was a boy who wore three-piece leisure suits—in the third grade! One time he wore a powder blue tuxedo to a school assembly. It was a mystery to me how or where he got his clothes. It definitely wasn't the same place my mother bought mine. I think Andre got some of Uncle BooKay's old hand-me-down threads. He had all flavor of shoes, hats, and leather or suede coats, plus fly belts.

Andre's ensembles were legendary—mine, on the other hand, were laughable. He showed up to class looking like Superfly, while I wore a Superman Underoos T-shirt and a pair of Braxtons blue jeans to school. Ever hear of Braxtons? Most people haven't. I think they only manufactured three or four pairs. My mother bought me two of them. I always assumed they were the cheapest bootleg blue jeans on the market. You couldn't wear white athletic socks or underwear with Braxtons because by the end of the school day, they would be light blue from all the dye that bled out of them.

In all honesty, I was a slob as a young boy. I'd pick out my curly Afro once in the morning and after that it was on its own. Many mornings we'd play a game of tackle football before school and I'd walk into homeroom sweating with bleeding Braxtons, dirty Kroger's sneakers, my small-medium T-shirt (we called them smediums) with leaves and twigs sticking out of my Jesse Jackson.

Andre and I are four years apart, so just as he was leaving a school, I was entering it. His was a tough act to follow. Not only was Andre *GQ* Teen of the Year, but he was also always the "most likely" this or the "best" that. Mr. Perfect. And if that wasn't enough, the boy could also sing...very well.

"That boy sho can sang!" was a phrase often uttered after he'd belt out some song in church. Of course, Andre was a regular at church, too. I think he got baptized the day after he got christened. My devilish ass, on the other hand, joined church at fifteen, and that was mostly to qualify for a church-sponsored summer retreat that boasted a girl/guy ratio of eight to one. (I broke at least four commandments that summer.) But not Andre. Though he probably just didn't get caught, because he had plenty of girls. That's another area where I couldn't compete: if his girls were dimes, mine were nickels.

After embarrassing Andre one day by my mere presence, he sat me down and gave it to me straight, no chaser.

"Baby bro, if you're going to hang out with me, you have to get yourself together." His gaze was pitiful.

I looked down at my flannel pajama shirt and green carpenter pants, which came with a belt loop big enough to hold a sledgehammer. I know what you're thinking: No, I didn't walk around with a hammer in that loop. How stupid would that look? That loop is where I carried my house and bicycle lock keys. Anyway, I looked down and said, of course, "What's wrong with what I'm wearing?"

"Byron, you look like a janitor."

Andre gave me a few of his old clothes and then took me to Ned Brothers, his barber. Ned's was where all the real players got their fades hooked up. This was the big league. Naps were not allowed in Ned's. Up until that point, I didn't even know that I had what was called "good" hair. It didn't matter to me. Hair was just something that was on your head.

Anyway, after a seven-dollar haircut and half a handful of Royal Crown pomade, I had enough waves in my hair to go surfing. When I showed up at school the following Monday, my teachers and classmates thought I was a new student. Oh, I was full of myself after that. Even the light-skin girls were smiling at me now.

One of them was a freckle-faced cutie-pie named Cassandra, who had lips that would have pissed off Angelina Jolie. Cassandra was in the eighth grade but had a college-freshman body, the kind of the girl mothers warned their sons about. Too bad the week I met Cassandra, my mother and I weren't on speaking terms. One warm Friday evening in May at a school dance, we sat in the bleachers with all the other young couples. They were all huggin' and smoochin' as Atlantic Starr's "Send for Me" played over the gymnasium's cheap loudspeakers. Now, I was a world-champion hugger. In fact, that night I frisked Cassandra like I was store security and she was a shoplifter. But I didn't kiss her—honestly, I had never kissed a girl before. But that night, I was with an experienced lip-locker. It was no secret that Cassandra's mouth had been on more lips than Maybelline. I sat there in the bleachers feeling stupid until Cassandra, who was sitting between my legs, looked up and started kissing me. Whoa Nelly! I bounced around on those big lips like they were inner tubes. Before I knew it, I was kissing her forehead. On Monday morning, Cassandra casually mentioned to a few of her close girlfriends in her homeroom that Byron Harmon couldn't kiss. Her few close friends then casually mentioned to the *whole damn school* that Byron Harmon couldn't kiss. I was crushed, humiliated, nearly suicidal with embarrassment. It took every ounce of fortitude to walk around school after that episode.

But I was coming along.

**M**Y FATHER WAS MY HERO. WHILE MY OTHER FRIENDS LOOKED UP to movie stars or sports figures, I worshiped my father, warts and all. Our relationship became a lot more complicated during my teenage years, but as kid, I was his shadow.

My father spent a lot of time with me and I cherished every moment. We didn't do normal stuff like play catch in the park or hit baseballs. Pops wasn't a big sports fan—unless it was wrestling or boxing. He loved to watch "the fights," and he didn't care if it was Ali versus Frazier or the Junkyard Dog against two blind midgets. Pops liked westerns and war movies, too. He called them "shoot 'em ups," and I'd sit beside him drinking red Kool-Aid while he drank Schlitz and watched movies for hours.

The main thing we did together was go fishing. Pops was a serious angler. He was a member of a black fishing club called the Big Cypress Bass Hustlers, a group of guys who held tournaments and banquets that gave out awards like "Best Rod" or "Hustler of the Year." I thought they were awards for distinguished pimps.

My father had top-notch rods and reels and a tackle box that would have made Bill Dance jealous. He had everything in that box, from rubber worms to spinning lures to all kinds of weights and hooks. His boat was equipped with sonar and depth-finding devices. The fish didn't stand a chance. We'd wake up long before daybreak on Saturday mornings. It started with the knock.

"Get your ass up. It's ain't your birthday."

I'd wipe the sleep from eyes and look out the window, then at my watch.

29

*3:30 am?* All of sudden I would become a charter member of People for the Ethical Treatment of Animals.

"Pops, I don't feel like killing any fish today."

Pops would push open the door with extreme force, slamming it against the wall. "Boy, get your black ass out of that bed before I put my foot in it. Breakfast is on the table."

My father never fully explained his Army duties to me, but for the sake of his comrades in Vietnam, I hope he wasn't a cook. On the table was a hot heaping plate of… something. It looked like ground beef mixed with thick horse urine slathered over burnt cocker spaniel's ass.

"What's this?" I asked.

He looked down proudly. "Boy, in 'Nam we called that S.O.S."

I gingerly poked my fork into the soft, oozing center. "S.O.S.?"

"Yeah," Pops smiled. "Shit on a Shingle."

I threw my fork down. "I see why we lost the war."

Once on the road we had to stop at a convenience store and stock up on stuff like ice, drinks, and cold cuts. Obviously, my father didn't care what he ate or drank. But I did. I'd race to the store's back aisle where the snacks were. There I'd be, licking my lips in ravenous anticipation of the Little Debbies, Twinkies, or Marshmallow Moon Pies. My father would walk right by me like I was invisible.

"Here, hold this," he would order.

Dejected, I looked down at the thick pack of lunchmeat. "Ugh, Liverwurst?"

"Shut up. Starving kids in Africa would love to eat this."

"Well, let's donate this pack to them."

Pops laughed. He liked a good comeback line. "Okay, okay get yourself a pack of bologna."

"Bologna? I want ham."

Pops reached into his pocket and felt around. "Looks like I don't have any ham money. But I got bologna money."

We primarily fished for bass and we always caught a nice batch to bring home for my mother to fry.

"Catch and release my ass," Pops would joke. "We're eating this."

I will always remember my time with Pops on the water, just the two of us, talking and laughing for hours. On one of those fishing trips he gave me what turned out to be some of the best advice I ever received. When

I was in the seventh grade, I was sweet on this little girl named Diana. Brown-skinned with long permed curls, she was an early bloomer—a very womanly looking little girl. All the boys called her Princess Di. I used to write her little love notes and tape them to her locker. The notes were little poems that I had scribbled on late nights listening to oldies on the local "quiet storm" radio station. Diana loved those notes. She fell for me hard, and my head was swollen.

"You have such a way with words," Diana told me one day during lunch.

I just smiled. After all, I did have a way with words. The problem was they were other people's words. The notes were nothing more than verses from classic R&B songs sung by The Isley Brothers, LTD, and Barry White. I'd just change them up a little bit. Well, I fooled Diana, but her mom must have been listening to the same station, because she found one of my notes and cross-examined Diana about the source.

"My friend Byron wrote that," she defended me.

I can imagine her mother frowning pitifully at her naive young daughter: "Yeah, Byron and Teddy Pendergrass."

The next day Diana stormed into Mrs. Gray's homeroom class, where I was holding court, and threw her stack of poems at me. The sound of the class laughing at me still stings to this day.

I told Pops the story one day while we were fishing, and after nearly spitting up his Schlitz from laughing so hard, he looked me in the eye and said, "Son, you have to be original. Write what's in your heart."

From then on, I did. It's a mantra I live my life by. I'd give anything for just one more of those Saturdays. Just me and my daddy. Pops taught me so much about life, about how to be a man.

That summer would be one of the last times before we became more like enemies than father and son.

I WASN'T AROUND IN 1967, BUT I KNOW ONE THING: 1984 WAS MY OWN personal "Summer of Love." In three short, hot months, I lost my virginity, smoked my first joint, started working, and finally had some money in *my* pocket. After that summer, I would never be the same.

I became cool. I was now going to high school, and not just any high school. I was going to Washington Marion, the hippest, blackest, ghetto-est high school in the city. We had the best of everything at Washington Marion—the best football team, the best marching band, the best basketball team, and the best brawls. Our motto was, "If we lose the game, don't worry: we'll win the fight."

The school's nickname was K-MART, which stood for Killers, Murderers, Arsonists, Rapists, and Thieves. Before I graduated, each one of those crimes had been committed at Washington Marion. At this K-MART, the only blue light specials were the blue lights of the police cruisers that routinely raced to the school. There were other monikers the school had to shake off. One of the saddest was the Maternity Ward, because at least fifteen girls seemed to be pregnant at all times.

It was just one of many sad indictments of our school system. I felt totally unprepared academically while I was in school. I did more personal reading than I did homework. Half of our textbooks were woefully out of date. The white schools in town had vastly superior facilities, better funding, and far less crime. With razor-sharp concertina wire rimming the school's fence, Washington Marion was like a prison.

Presiding over all of this madness was the warden himself, Roscoe

Moore. Roscoe was the rawest educator I've ever heard of—and he had to be. He would curse a student out in a heartbeat. Roscoe stood about 6'3", weighed over 300 pounds, and was mean as a middle linebacker. As head principal, he'd stand outside his office, pat his perfect Afro, and wait for the bell to ring. Heaven help you if you were tardy or even just walked slow.

"Hey little nig," Roscoe would bark, looking at his watch. "Get cha' ass to class."

But if you were a cute girl, you could crawl to class.

"Hey, baby," he'd purr, waving.

Luckily, as a freshman I didn't have to deal with Roscoe just yet. Washington Marion was split into two locations. One campus was less than a mile from my house on Guinn Street. That's where freshman went. Sophomores, juniors, and seniors went to the campus across town with Roscoe. Just before I started my freshman year, the local school board decided to merge a bunch of schools, most of them black. Lake Charles High and Boston High became Lake Charles Boston High. Washington High and Marion High became...well, you know the rest. However, the school board didn't seem to know or care that all of these schools had previously hated each other. There were huge fights at both of the newly combined schools and the rivalry between LCB and Washington Marion took on the significance of the Union versus the Confederacy.

As freshmen, we were spared the brunt of combat. We were all by ourselves at the old Marion High location. Well, not totally alone. We shared the school with special education students. Some of these "kids" were far older, bigger, meaner, and more violent than even the baddest of us regular high-schoolers.

The Special Ed students were normally segregated in a separate part of the school; their short yellow bus even arrived at school a half-hour after we were in our first class. But every so often, one of them would wander through the hallways during business hours. If you were a smart teacher, you made sure that when the last kid came into class you shut your door, then locked it. Then barricaded it. An open door was an open invitation. If you were tardy, you were out of luck and to brave it in the hallway. You became Theseus in the Minotaur's maze.

**M**Y FRESHMAN YEAR WAS ALSO THE YEAR THAT MY GPA SANK LIKE the *Titanic*. Tragically, I had brought home my first C, in algebra, no less. Mathematics was a subject in which I normally excelled.

"What the hell is this?" Pops demanded to know. He waved the yellow report card in my face like he was trying to cool me off.

I smiled like a man who knew things Pops didn't. "Uh, the C means that I was the class algebra champ."

"Champ my ass—more like chump," he frowned.

Pop's raised his right hand to pimp-slap me, but thought better of it and instead placed me under "house arrest" for the next six weeks. And Pops meant it. I could not leave the house, except for school or church or family obligations, for six solid weeks. I even had to put my neighborhood lawn-cutting business on hold, which destroyed my bank account. I'd had my heart set on buying a new pair of leather Dr. J Converse All-Stars. So far, I had saved fifteen of the twenty-four dollars I needed to buy them.

So I started sneaking out my bedroom window after my father went to sleep. I'd ride my bike across town and hang out with Little Harold, Craig, and Nelson, drinking beer all night and competing to see who could memorize the most lyrics from The Sugar Hill Gang's "Rapper's Delight," the first smash-hit rap song, which had our local radio in a chokehold all year long. Most of my friends were smoking marijuana by then, but I wasn't ready to take that plunge yet. After getting a good buzz off Budweiser, I'd ride my bike back home drunk.

I got away with it for about a week. Then one night I was crawling back through my window when I heard an unmistakable voice yell, "Freeze, motherfucker!"

I froze, hands up, heart racing. "Daddy, it's me, Byron."

Pops flipped the light switch. Light flooded the room.

*Oh, God, I don't want to die,* I thought. I was staring down the barrel of a loaded .38 special. I was scared sober—but not Pops. He was blitzed out of his mind, probably from his favorite, Crown Royal.

"I was about to shoot your black *assss,*" he slurred. "I thought you were a burger-larrr."

That incident scared me straight and ended my late night creeps, but it was the opening salvo in what would become a not-so-cold war between Pops and me. The biggest bone of contention between us was my declining grades. Up until that point, my report cards had been pristine things of beauty, usually one long column of A's. I never hesitated to bring my report card home to my parents. From the first grade until my freshman year in high school, I had made only five Bs. I had been in the Honor Society, Student Council, and 4-H—a veritable pillar of the community, the kind of young man parents would allow their daughter to study with alone in her bedroom, with the door closed and the music turned up.

Why, in the third grade I was one of a handful of students from my school to be selected for SPARK, a city-wide gifted students program. The program brought together students from different schools in the area twice a week, where we were taught things like chess, art history, advanced science, and even early computer programming like BASIC and FORTRAN.

Our Socrates was Barbara Bachrach, a motivated educator who lectured us on ancient philosophies and took us on exciting and sobering field trips to places like the Johnson Space Center in Houston and former slave plantations in New Orleans. With her help, we read books like Machiavelli's *The Prince*, Clausewitz's *On War*, and Sun Tzu's *Art of War*. That was some deep stuff for teenagers. Students could participate in SPARK from the third through eighth grades. SPARK gave me a tremendous edge on my fellow classmates and access to knowledge and information that shaped my whole outlook on life. I might have remained a straight-A student if SPARK lasted through high school.

One big subject that we didn't learn about in SPARK was drug abuse. My grades started getting lower right around the time I started to drink and get high. At first, I blamed my decline on the demands of playing for the junior varsity football team, on which I started at right guard. However, I rarely went to practice, so that defense had a gaping hole in it.

It was the mid-1980s, and Nancy Reagan's weak "just say no" commercials were all over the news. The first lady's sappy campaign didn't stand a chance at rowdy Washington Marion. We had our own slogan, "There ain't no way we can say nope to dope."

It wasn't overt peer pressure that started me down the slippery slope. Even though my entire neighborhood was smoking, no one pressured me to get high. In fact, Damon, a friend of mine who also sold drugs, initially turned me down when I first asked to buy a "white girl," a term we used to describe loose joints. We were standing by the back walkway behind the cafeteria, which served as an unofficial hoods' hang out.

"B., you don't want to do this," Damon warned, his eyes darting, always on the lookout for a teacher or a narc.

I was unfazed. "C'mon, Damon."

But Damon was a drug dealer with a heart of gold. "I can't do it, B.," he admitted rather sheepishly. "You're...you're my boy."

"Dog, I ain't trying to buy heroin, I just want some weed."

"I can't do it, B.," he frowned.

"Okay," I said, walking off in the direction of a competing drug dealer. "Black Terrance is selling two white girls for three dollars."

Damon, ever the businessman, countered, "In that case, I'll give you three for five."

Later that evening, I sat on the back steps of our house and kissed my first white girl. At first, I gave that white girl just a tiny peck on the cheek, but pretty soon we were French kissing, my tongue all down her throat. I knew Pops would lynch me for kissing a white girl, but my desire to taste her forbidden fruit was too strong. White girls would become the death of little black boys like myself.

Three minutes later I felt like I had inhaled the secrets of the universe. I lost all track of space and time. I was out of Earth's atmosphere and beyond its gravitational pull. I held the joint away from my mouth, stared at it, and then let it go. The joint floated in the air like a hot air balloon, the lit end flickering in the dark like a firefly. I grabbed it back and smiled. I looked down at my dog Herman, a pit bull. I could have sworn that he winked his eye at me. It was as if I had found the Holy Grail or the alchemists' fabled philosopher's stone. I truly felt that at that moment if I'd had a calculator, pen, and pad, I could have cured cancer.

From that night on I smoked weed nearly every day until I graduated from high school. Thanks to sleeping most of the time and only doing half my homework, I finished off my freshman year with four more C's, but not before brawling with Charles Brewer in the boy's bathroom over a lost bet. That got me a warning from school officials. But it was when I let one of my friends borrow my backpack, and he got caught with some brass knuckles, a *Penthouse* magazine, and a bottle of Mad Dog 20/20, that the proverbial feces hit the fan. My co-defendant snitched me out, and I got suspended from school.

My father had to come to school to get me, and since he was a deputy sheriff and was wearing his full uniform, half the school thought I was going to jail. I wished that I were, because when we got home Pops pretty much beat the black off me.

My suspension was part of a larger problem. I was really starting to act out. Most of it could probably be blamed on the massive amounts of drugs and alcohol I was consuming, but I also had to see and hear things in the street about my father that made me despise him. I knew he was out there drinking and philandering but trying to tell me to do right. Pure hypocrisy. Many a night we'd drunkenly stare at each across the dinner table, both of us red-eyed. My mother would sneer and stare at us like aliens.

"Son, you know I lovvve you," Pops would slur. "Why are you hooked on that stuff?"

I sucked my teeth. "What stuff?"

"Drugs," he sighed.

"You're the one hooked on drugs," I countered.

Uh-oh. He began staring daggers at me.

"You know I'm right. You smoke cigarettes—that's nicotine, a drug. You're the one who's an alcoholic and a drug addict."

In a fit of rage, he knocked his chair over and grabbed me by the collar, his face only inches away from mine. I winced from smell of liquor on his breath. "Fuck ya mean I'ma acka-oholic?"

"Daddy, you can drink a case of beer in one sitting."

"So?"

I'd stare at him with a look of utter disgust and waited for him to hit me, but he didn't. He sat back in the chair and cried. I really wanted to punch him, but I wouldn't dare fight my daddy, because he told me once very sternly, "Boy, if you ever raise your hands against me, I will kill you." I believed him, too.

I also finished my freshman year deflowered.

Her name was Charmagne, but because of the way she made me feel all bubbly inside, her name should have been Champagne. Charmagne lived around the block from Guinn Street, and it was as if she was fine china or something, because she'd only be out on special occasions. We'd kiss for a half-hour at a time. Her lips were the New World, and I was Christopher Columbus. Whenever we were alone I had to touch some part of her body. After a few weeks of going out we had done everything except have sex. I was really scared.

The real thing went down on a warm afternoon in July. Little girls were outside playing Double Dutch and the bell of the Good Humor man echoed through the neighborhood. It was one of those days when you just knew something good was going to happen. I raced my Schwinn toward her house like I was Lance Armstrong.

I was so excited I nearly crashed my bike into Charmagne's house. I rang the doorbell and she answered the door wearing tight blue shorts and a tank top. She kissed me as soon I stepped into the living room and wasted no time leading me to her bedroom. When she took off her clothes I wanted to take off running. My heart was pounding like a jackhammer.

I gently, if somewhat clumsily, laid her down on the bed and began kissing her, but she was through with kissing; she wanted me to make love to her. I was so nervous, I couldn't for the life of me figure out how to do it properly. Charmagne wanted me to run my fingers all over her body—but I was all thumbs.

"That's not it," she said on more than one occasion.

"Oops," was all I could say in response.

Frustrated, she finally said, "Let me do it."

"I don't have a condom," I mumbled.

She frowned. "You don't need one."

For the next six minutes I died and entered the bosom of Heaven. I went toward the light. Then it happened—I arrived. Fireworks exploded, angels began to sing, and trumpets blared. A jolt of pure electricity flowed through my veins. Then in a flash it went away.

My legs were so wobbly I had to walk beside my bike all the way home.

I went straight to the bathroom and looked at my reflection in the mirror. I looked the same, felt the same, but I wasn't—I felt like a man now. I felt ten feet tall. I knew the secret handshake. I had "just got laid" written all over my face. And then, I threw up.

THE FIRST DAY OF CLASS MY SOPHOMORE YEAR, I WAS SCARED TO DEATH. Walking onto the main campus of Washington Marion, you couldn't help notice that the school had a penitentiary look and feel to it. An imposing gated fence topped by rolls of concertina wire encircled the campus. I exited the school bus and saw the throngs of thugs hanging out—future felons who had names like "Two Sweet," "Killer-Bean," and "Boogie" eyed my new back-to-school Converse the way hungry lions eyed zebras.

Mornings at Washington Marion often took on the air of an adventure. If you were to visit the campus during this era, before you even walked through the back doors (students rarely entered through the front, at least the cool ones didn't), you'd first have to dodge a gauntlet of tricked out cars equipped with ear-splitting sound systems blasting classic rap songs like Whodini's "Friends" or UTFO's "Roxanne, Roxanne."

A cloud of marijuana smoke hovered over the walkway like LA smog. That's where I'd be, of course. There, you'd find the crème de le crème of the school's drug trade, guys like Telvis G., Alfred, and the Calcasieu Street boys hawking their wares to eager customers.

"Three for Fives right 'chere!"

"Got dat skunk!"

"Dime bags!"

Glancing around the schoolyard, you'd see cliques with names like *Me Phi Me*, a "wannabe" pretty-boy Greek fraternity whose members often performed step shows at dances or during our lunch hour. Most of the other male students hated them, of course.

And if you listened closely you'd overhear Killa Bean (a member of

*G Phi G,* aka Gangster Phi Gangster), plotting to jump members of Me Phi Me. G Phi G, whose members came from the ranks of Washington Marion's top thugs, defended the school's honor all over town, especially if rivals visited our campus to talk to our girls. G Phi G's hospitality was hostile. One famous after-school brawl ended with a shotgun blast to the back windows of a truck occupied by some guys from LaGrange High.

Once inside the school, your eyes would feast on beauties like Yolanda Washington, a tall, leggy, light-skinned lovely strutting down the hallway as if it were a runway. Or your eyes would literally pop out of their sockets at the sight of Tammy Diamond, Vicki Sylvester, Kim Washington, or Tasha Henderson, teenagers in grown women's bodies. These girls were amazons with figures that could easily earn them top dollar at any gentleman's club on the planet.

Posted up in front of a mirror in his locker would be Larry Leday or Randy "Jive" Jordan, spritzing obscene amounts of activator all over their extra long Jheri-curls. Linguists would also shake their heads trying to understand the conversation being carried on near the water fountain between Donald Glodd and Wayne Price, self-proclaimed student-pimps who invented their own language.

"Yima better Kreet Dat Sheet Bwoy," Donald would say, holding a firm grip on his crotch.

Wayne, wearing his customary tight Levi's and Stacy Adams shoes, would then suck his teeth and roll his eyes before mumbling, "Dat Bee-yotch Can Yee My Yak Alone."

By chance if you wandered into the boys bathroom, you'd first catch a contact buzz from all of the herb smoke, but would more than likely be treated to a hilarious session of "The Dozens" featuring Greg "Hollywood" Henderson and his cousin Sly, a dead ringer for Jimi Hendrix.

"Greg, your momma's so fat she has to iron her clothes in the driveway," Sly would crack.

"Heh!" Greg would grunt in his trademark chuckle, "Whatever. Your room is soooo small, I stretched out on your bed and my feet were on top of the dresser."

Primping by their lockers and comparing outfits would be Althea Duriseau and Nicole Willis, two of my best female friends and well-known fashion plates. "The Twins," as they were called, were known for their beauty and their clothes. They often came to school dressed in identical outfits.

And already in class and on the verge of combining the Pythagorean theorem with a yet-to-be-invented algorithm would be Shannon Johnson, future valedictorian.

This was a whole new experience for us. As freshmen, we had been spoiled, coddled even. We had our own school building, and our freshman football and basketball teams had gone undefeated. Cocky and full of ourselves, we were determined to repeat our success at the next level. Meanwhile, the varsity teams had just come off of a dismal season and had basically waited all summer long for the chance to murder us.

On our first day at practice, the seniors jumped the sophomores, beat us up, and dragged us through the mud. Then it really got bad. By the end of the week, I had my first major fight with the team bully. Ironically his name was Harmon, first name Leo, though he was no relation. Leo would spit on, slap, and generally terrorize any weaker player who wouldn't kiss his fat ass. He had already broken one guy's arm. It was only a matter of time before we crossed paths. I won't lie, I was scared shitless. Leo was huge, a big fat nasty blob of evil.

One afternoon during practice, after our coach would whistle a play dead, the seniors would continue to hit and tackle us sophomores. Even players sitting on the bench were assaulted. You never knew where the hit was coming from, and the coaches would just look the other way. A player's head had to be on a swivel at all times. After one particular play, I spotted Leo barreling toward me like a raging bull. At the last second before he made impact I turned and punched Leo in his balls. He folded over like a new wallet. Next, I sort of blacked out. Later, I was told I'd gone berserk—I grabbed Leo in a headlock and slammed all 300 pounds of his whale-like blubber head-first into the dirt, then kicked him. When I came to, half the team was giving me high-fives. In the locker room after practice, Leo tried to save face and taunt me, but I casually showed him the butcher knife I'd brought to school in my book bag, and I had no more problems out of him—or anyone else for that matter. Word spread around school quickly. With this one act, I had earned respect, one of the few sophomores who had.

I was a decent player, but I hated football. No—what I hated was football practice. I skipped practice so often, the equipment guy cleaned out my locker nearly every week, thinking I had quit the team. The main reason I hated practice was because I hated hanging my flashy clothes in those dirty lockers. For me, school was a daily fashion show and I didn't want to get the few outfits I had dirty. By this time, my brother Andre, the fashion plate, had given me a leg up in the form of his hand-me-downs. And I was definitely trying to avoid showering with any of those upperclassmen/ inmates. I felt that I was too fly to practice, so mostly I just showed up for the games and warmed the bench.

However, there were benefits to playing football *that year*, 1985, which was the year that my neighbor Nelson Joseph became a bona fide superstar. Our team was undefeated thanks to his heroics as a wide receiver. Mark Cole, our quarterback, had a rocket for an arm. The two routinely combined for three to six touchdowns per game. We blew teams out by 40 and 50 points. Nelson's stats were gaudy. After the games, he would stand outside the stadium signing autographs with some of the school's hottest dimes hanging on his arm. We happily accepted Nelson's cast-offs—hell, even they were at least eights.

Nelson's feats were all performed in front of tens of thousands of fanatical fans on Friday nights. All over the south, people are *serious* about their high school football. But our school stood out, at least in Lake Charles. People from other schools would skip their own teams' games to come to ours. One game at our stadium had nearly 20,000 screaming people in the stands. Folks bought brand-new outfits just to wear to the games.

One of the highlights of the game was halftime—that's when our band performed. It was almost unfair how funky our marching band was. Huck, the tall, lanky band director, was related to Dr. Isaac Greggs, the legend who led the famous "human jukebox" marching band at Southern University, a historically black college in Baton Rouge. Instead of traditional marching band songs, Southern's band played whatever was on the radio at the time. Their routines became our band's routines. We copied everything from them, from the capes on the band members' uniforms to the frontline of twenty "dancing dolls." The way those leotard-clad beauties high-stepped and swiveled their hips was enough to give an old man a heart attack. When our band marched onto the field, people would be dancing in the stands.

If you were on the football team, even a scrub like myself, you were golden. Even I was dating a senior flag captain in our marching band. Her name was Tanzi Edwards. Charmagne had recently dumped me, but since this is my book, let me go on record by saying that I had outgrown her. After all, she was just a freshman. Anyway, our team could not be stopped all that year. Our regular-season record was 14-0, and we made it all the way to the state championships, which were held in the New Orleans Superdome. The football team was excused from classes so that we could go to New Orleans a week early. *First mistake.* We weren't in our hotels two hours before there was a drug bust in one of our player's rooms. I had just left the room and narrowly escaped getting caught in the dragnet. The players involved were scrubs, so it wasn't too big a deal to the team, but it was a harbinger of what was to come.

On the day of the championship game, most of our team members were stoned. *Second mistake.* Lord knows I was high as a car note on a new Bentley. I had no chance of getting in the game, so it didn't matter to me, but it should have mattered to our starters. In front of 30,000 people, we got our asses kicked by John Curtis, a powerhouse outfit composed of Neanderthal-looking white boys. Even their water boys were on steroids. After that game, I retired from football for good. It was time to make some money.

If I was to have any chance of ever having another sexual experience, one that I didn't have to pay for, I needed a paycheck to upgrade my wardrobe. I had exhausted Andre's supply of hand-me-downs. Besides my brother was very skinny and I...wasn't. I have been called a lot of things in my life, but skinny has never been one of them. It didn't help that Pops was pressuring me to start "contributing."

"Pops, I'm fifteen," I reminded him.

He sucked his teeth and rolled his eyes. "You should thank your Momma, I wanted your ass to start working last year."

But in December of 1985, the job market for a fifteen-year-old in Lake Charles was pretty bleak. I begged my mother to get me a job at Piccadilly's, the cafeteria-style restaurant where she worked. It should have been called Harmon's, because Andre also worked there along with three of our cousins. Clearly, Shirley was a fan of nepotism. Right?

Wrong.

"No," she declared emphatically, denying me an honest livelihood.

*Okay, whatever,* I thought. *I'm not going to beg her. I got my pride, after all.*

But Christmas was right around the corner, and if I couldn't get Tanzi a present, I would have no chance of unwrapping *her.* Who the hell needs pride?

"Please, Momma, please, I'm begging you, please get me a job."

"Boy, you don't want to wash no pots," she warned.

She was right, I *didn't* want to wash pots, but beggars can't be choosy. "I'll do it, Momma, I don't care."

"All right," she relented. "But don't embarrass me."

*Thanks for the vote of confidence*, I thought.

The next day, which was a Friday, my mother came home from work and handed me a bag. It contained an authentic Piccadilly work shirt. It resembled the shirts worn by UPS drivers today.

"You start Monday," my mother deadpanned.

"What's my schedule?" I asked, barely able to contain my glee. Pops, who was sitting on the couch watching the local news, turned his head and stared at me pitifully.

"C'mon, what's my schedule, Momma?" I badgered her.

She sighed, growing weary of my excitement. "Monday through Thursday, 5 to 9 pm."

Yes, I thought, rubbing my hands together excitedly. I looked up at the ceiling and started calculating. *That means I'll be off on the weekends.* "How much do I get paid?"

"Three twenty-five," my mother said, sitting down to rub her aching feet.

I started jumping up and down with joy. "Three hundred and twenty-five dollars a week? I'm rich."

Pops shook his head in disgust. "That's three-dollars and twenty-five cents an hour, *dumbass.*"

My arms fell to my sides like somebody shot me. "Three dollars?" I asked. The paltry amount tasted like cough syrup in my mouth. "There's no way I'm washing pots for that kind of chump change."

Three days later, I was surrounded by more steel than a skyscraper. I had never seen so many dirty pots in my life. I stood there, clad in my official Piccadilly's short- sleeved shirt, white apron, and paper sailor hat, in front of the biggest sink on the planet. The red tiled floor all around me was soaking wet, and I had to hold on to the sink just to keep from breaking my neck. It was hot as hell in that kitchen, too.

One after another, the dirty pots kept piling up. All sizes, containing all manner of delicacies. I was dazzled by the selection of stylish stainless steel cookware. There were large soup pots, medium rice pots, long flat bread pans, gigantic stew pots, heavy black skillets caked with fish and chicken grease,

and pots that contained what could only have been radioactive plutonium.
*What have I gotten myself into?* I asked of God.

"Hey you, wake up," a voice startled me out of my trance. It was A.J.,
the manager. "We're out of clean pots. C'mon, quit lollygagging."

"Huh?" I mumbled. I was overwhelmed. I looked around at the other
workers in the kitchen for a sign of sympathy. There was none. I had to sink
or swim on my own.

"Three-bucks and twenty-five funky-ass cents, huh?" I muttered before
diving in.

Hours later, I was still bustin' suds. My first night on the job and already
I was receiving overtime. Not because I volunteered for it, but because I
couldn't finish my work on time. I scrubbed my last pot at 11:45 pm. I
slumped over the sink, spent. I shuffled to the parking lot, exhausted. Pops,
my driver, was outside waiting in the car, snoring.

I knocked on the passenger side window.

He snorted and reached over to unlock the door. I plopped into the
front seat, leaned back, and closed my eyes, too tired to cry. Pops stared at
me.

"Well?" he asked, rubbing sleep from his eyes.

"I quit," I admitted rather sheepishly.

My father's eyes flashed bright as 100-watt light bulbs. "What did you
say?"

I cleared my throat. "I, um, uh, I q-q-quit."

See, by the time I was fifteen I was well versed in the art of quitting.
The list of things I had quit was long: Boy Scouts, Little League, football,
karate lessons. I'd even quit the basketball team before the coach made the
first cut. Quitting had become a way of life.

Pops was having none of it. I could quit anything except a job that paid
real money. After all, it was time to pay tribute—I mean, contribute. Pops
made one of his meanest faces. "Tomorrow afternoon, your black ass will
either be working at Piccadilly or laying in the hospital."

Needless to say, after saying a short prayer, I got out of the car and
walked back into the restaurant and un-quit. Eventually I went to war on
those pots. I developed a style that was both graceful yet functional. My
time at the sink taught me one of my first and most important life lessons—
that with hard work and dedication I could handle adversity, stress, and
pressure. That was the last time I quit anything.

**M**ARK JOHNSON WAS ONLY A SOPHOMORE, BUT HE WAS THE STAR running back of our undefeated varsity football team. Dark, compact, and heavily muscled, Johnson was the kind of bruising runner who, once he was sprung from the line of scrimmage and free in the open field, immediately started looking for a cornerback or safety to run over. They usually ran for cover. One time Johnson was less than ten yards away from a touchdown when he turned around and charged at the chasing defensive players like a raging bull. After wiping out two of the pursuers, he turned back around and casually strolled into the end zone. But one afternoon during school lunch, Johnson's feet failed him.

The little bit of what we saw out the back window of Mrs. Carter's Algebra II class blew our minds—and these were minds already conditioned to regular violence. There was always some type of disturbance going on at Washington Marion, but mostly it was your garden-variety gang fight, or a jealous boyfriend slamming his unfaithful girlfriend's head into a locker. That kind of stuff wouldn't rate a mention in the school paper. However, the star running back being hotly pursued by Poppa, an extremely disgruntled student who was trying to carve his initials into Johnson's back with a switchblade, was enough to make us put our pencils down.

"Yo, look," yelled Tyrone Ned, whose desk (and GPA) put him at the very back of the class, thus giving him a bird's eye view of the impending carnage.

Mrs. Carter's fleshy cheeks flushed red. "Oh my goodness. *Class, don't look.*"

Class, don't look? Of course we looked.

"Ooh, Poppa's stabbing him," pointed out Zeke, a normally not-so-bright sixth-year senior. But this time Zeke was right on the money. As the two rounded the bend by our window, Johnson faltered for a split second. Maybe it was his Stacy Adams pointy-toed oxfords and tight Levi's that hindered him from reaching top speed, or maybe it was the loss of blood. Anyway, it was enough time for Poppa to slice Johnson's T-shirt into a tank top. Johnson managed to struggle free, knock away the knife, then limp away at record speed. The whole scene lasted less than thirty seconds. It reminded me of a botched lion attack on a zebra.

Mrs. Carter didn't miss a beat. She tapped her piece of chalk on the board. "Okay class, who wants to factor this trinomial?"

Word on the street had it that Johnson had been caught with Nicole, Poppa's vivacious girlfriend. Word on the street also had it that Nicole's head was soon scheduled for a date with a locker. Such was life at K-MART. There was another stabbing the following week, this time in a boys' bathroom. Some guy got it in the neck and stumbled into the hallway, blood spurting like a geyser.

Later, speedy Mark Johnson—a guy I'd gone to school with since middle school—would eventually be convicted of raping a white girl. He was sentenced to twenty years in Angola State Penitentiary. He wouldn't be the last of our fellow students to be incarcerated. After a football game, three of our other classmates beat another student to death with a baseball bat. Another alumnus got stabbed to death at the park by my house over a ham sandwich. His brother met the same fate at a teen club. You had to be really careful or really lucky to get out of Washington Marion unscathed.

But as I said, the students were used to it. We really didn't think about it much. At bottom, I think most of us felt that as long it wasn't us getting shot or stabbed, it didn't really register.

Meanwhile, I had my first serious heartbreak. A May-December relationship in high school is a bad idea. As a sophomore dating a hot senior, I was living way above my pay grade.

The dirty deed went down at a dance, the last dance of the football season. Everybody we knew was there. Why Tanzi chose such a public place to bump me off remains a mystery to me. The dance floor of Washington Marion's raggedy women's gymnasium was packed with hundreds of sweaty teenagers, some standing around looking cute, some dancing, and some conducting full body cavity searches on each other in darkened corners.

The pungent aroma of marijuana smoke filled the stale air. Meanwhile, DJ Kevin Nash on the one's and two's was spinning "Pac Jam," one of the era's biggest records, at ear-splitting volume.

I should have known something was up. Tanzi had been acting funny all week. But honestly, my nose so wide-open I wouldn't have noticed if my balls were on fire. There we were at the dance, a happy couple. I was standing behind Tanzi with my arms around her waist, grinning like a Cheshire cat. Every now and then I'd wink at one of my envious friends.

Then the "Buck" stopped here. His real name was Ernest Walker, but his nickname was Buck.

"What's up, B.?" Buck asked.

*Uh oh, what is his old ass doing here?* I thought, ignoring him. Buck was a classmate and friend of my brother Andre, but no friend of mine. Worst of all, he was a *college dude*. There were only three things that made me nervous back then: in this order, they were 1. acne, 2. oversized and overaged special-ed students, and 3. college dudes. They were always trying to lure our impressionable young girls. That was my job. The defense systems of mature high school girls are particularly vulnerable to a college dude attack, and Tanzi was a mature high school girl.

Buck lightly tapped my arm, attempting to get my attention. "I said, 'What up, B.?'"

"Chilling," I answered nonchalantly. "What's up with you?"

"Chilling," he responded, beady eyes darting in the dark, acting like he wasn't looking at my girl. I was standing behind Tanzi, so I couldn't see the way her beady eyes were eyeing him up and down.

"Who is this lovely lady?" he asked.

I paused, annoyed by his little charade but ever the gentleman. "Tanzi, Buck, Buck, Tanzi."

They shook hands, their fingers lingering a bit too long for my taste before Buck walked off. A short while later, Tanzi feigned some type of whatever and left the room. My envious friends wasted no time alerting me that Buck, my Brutus, had left, too. And there I was, like Caesar lying on the floor of the Senate, knifed through the heart. I was devastated and felt like a fool. For the next month, I moped around. In the end, though, it must have been for the best. Buck and Tanzi have been married now for nearly twenty years.

Oh well, what did I expect? How could a sophomore in high school compete with a college dude? What did I have to offer? I'd had to hitch a ride to the dance, I had a curfew, and I definitely could not afford a hotel.

And just like millions of jilted boyfriends before me, I decided to get serious about getting women. It was time to broaden my horizons. And by the end of the summer, I had found the best place to meet women: the Baptist church.

**F**OR THE NEXT FEW MONTHS, THOUGH, I FIRST TRIED MY BEST TO LEAVE a good-looking corpse. To dull the sharp pain of a love lost, I partied like it was 1999, even though it was still just 1985. I knew it was going to be a summer for the record books when I glimpsed my year-end report card.

Stricken with terror, I folded the card, then unfolded it and looked at it again, as if that would change the grades. *I'm a dead man.*

When it came to education, I'd always been a paradox. Ever since I was a preschooler, I had loved reading to gain knowledge. My love affair with the written word began with encyclopedias. I'd devoured entire sets by the time I exited Riverside Elementary. These included major volumes like the *Encyclopedia Britannica* and lesser works like *The Children's Book of Wonders*, plus dozens of other reference tomes on science, history, and biography. I was a wealth of useful and useless information.

I always found it odd that I had no desire for official school course work, but read for pleasure as if I were a librarian.

"You're the smartest dumb person I know," Pops used to joke.

In my spare time I was reading mystically oriented books like *Magister Ludi* by Hermann Hesse. Deep stuff—but I couldn't tell you what a dangling participle was. But I did know the alphabet, and I was getting dangerously close to mastering the fourth letter.

I made my very first D— make that two Ds, and the rest were Cs. Although I had passed to the eleventh grade, you didn't have to be Nostradamus to predict my father's reaction. Later on that afternoon, when

I presented the report card to Pops, my knees were shaking. Pops calmly unfolded the report card, scanned it, then without any trace of emotion calmly threw it on the table. "Well, it's official," he declared.

"What's official?"

"That you are a dumbass."

Through some weird stroke of luck, Pops didn't murder me. He didn't ground me, either. He basically threw in the towel. All he said was, "I'm giving up on you, son. When you graduate, find a new address."

So I basically checked out on life. I would go to work high. By that time I was a world-class pot washer, so it wasn't a big deal. That summer I went stark raving mad. I smoked weed, drank cheap wine, and lived recklessly on a daily basis. One night me, Dale, and Boobie Gallien dodged bullets shot by a crazy old white man after he caught us getting high in a field behind his house.

"Bzz! Bzz! Bzz!" The bullets whizzed over our heads like killer bees as we ducked behind Boobie's old Ford Ranger truck. When the old man went inside to reload, we hopped into the truck and sped off into the night, throwing empty Colt .45 bottles at his house.

This may sound twisted, but I am thankful I came of age before crack cocaine began its slow devastation. If I hadn't, I'm sure that right now I'd be a bona fide crackhead. Either that, or a dead ex-crackhead. Back then I was living way too fast to care. Every day was an adventure. Like the time the brakes crapped out on my friend Bubba's old clunker car and it crashed right through the front of a 7-11. We just jumped out laughing and took off running into the woods while the car sat idling in the middle of the potato chip aisle. One day I was on top of the world, the next day in the dirt. But thanks to a steady supply of chronic, I was always able to balance my lows with plenty of highs.

Run-DMC's *Raising Hell* was all the rage, and I was doing my best to act like a fourth member of the group. Although it began in the early '70s in the parks of the South Bronx, by the summer of '85 hip-hop was the dominant youth music in the country, especially in *da country*.

I wanted to be a rapper so bad. I went so far as starting a group with some of my homeboys. We called ourselves "The Lake City Boys." I was the leader, aka MC Shryme. You may be wondering—why did I call myself that?

*Because I talk a lot of shit/but it's all in a rhyme.*

*And when I put it all together/It spells Shryme.*

I know, I know, dammit, I know, but trust me, it was a hot nickname in 1985 for a teenager in Louisiana. Also in the group was my best friend Dale, aka Miny Mo. He didn't rap. Slim and handsome, he just stood off to one side of the stage posing as eye candy for the girls. Miny Mo could pull off the most outlandish outfits, too. One time he walked around the skating rink wearing a white silk tank top and Hawaiian print shorts, with a lavender bow tie around his neck. He looked like a chocolate Chippendale's dancer.

The other member of the group was my main man Bubba Stewart, aka SupaThug.

"Bubba Stewart in this beeyotch!" he used to scream at our shows, waving a plastic sub-machine gun (though sometimes he packed a real gun). A taller Wesley Snipes, Bubba was one of the most gangsterish dudes in the school. He routinely stored a pound of high-grade marijuana in his locker or a sawed-off shotgun in his trench coat. He was always either getting shot or shooting at somebody. Bubba gave us street cred and served as the group's beat boxer.

The last member and other rapper was San-Man. San-Man had the good fortune of being light-skinned just as it was coming into vogue. He was a devastating wordsmith, too. Our group won the freestyle battle three weeks in a row on KAOK, (aka 13K), a local AM station. As the so-called hot group, we had bull's-eyes on our backs with a lot of other wannabe rappers targeting us.

The cafeteria at lunchtime at Washington Marion became like "Showtime at the Apollo." Rappers squared off against each other across lunch tables and battled for supremacy. Students would cheer hot lines and mercilessly boo the losers. Our most memorable battle involved a crew fronted by Rick Bo, a class clown and formidable MC. It was tense in the cafeteria because Rick Bo's crew had been dissing San-Man all week. This was the first time they would rap face to face. The whole school was talking about it. It felt like Ali-Frazier III.

"Forget rappin', let me shoot 'em," Bubba pleaded.

"Please Bubba, don't shoot nobody today," I pleaded.

Another thing—no one knew that I was MC Shryme. People had only heard my voice on the radio, so when Rick Bo squared off against San-Man, I just silently stood to the side, the secret weapon. That day, I had skipped

English class to make my live debut. The cafeteria was quiet as midnight in a funeral home. Even Mrs. Edwards, the head cook, came out from the kitchen to listen. (Little did Mrs. Edwards know at the time, but her hairnet and wave cap would in later years become essential fashion accessories for gangsters worldwide.)

Rick Bo nearly killed San-Man with one shot. As his homie banged out a nasty beat on the lunch table, Rick Bo's head began bobbing like Ali in his prime. Once he locked in the groove, he began spittin'.

*"Yellow assed nigga/You ain't no brother."*

*"I saw you in the shower/You'se a white boy undercover."*

"Ooh," the crowd yelled. They were so loud their noise drowned out the rest of Rick Bo's rap. The last thing we heard had something to do with San-Man's mother and it rhymed with esophagus.

"Your turn," Rick Bo sneered.

San-Man looked at me. I looked away—toward the exit. But, thank God for Bubba Stewart. He began making music with his mouth.

"Boom Bap, Boom Boom Bap, Boom Bap, Boom Boom Bap," he beatboxed.

SupaThug was in the zone, and the way he was looping the beat, it sounded like an orchestra was in the room. The crowd looked around for the radio. Bubba's confidence was infectious. San-Man began searching for the hole in the loop. Once he located it, he began.

*"I'm the S-A-N-dash M-A-N"*

*"The SandMan from your dreams/ Here to rock again."*

*"You're out of your league/Rick, you lack experience."*

*"If rappin' was a sport/You'd be on the bench."*

The cafeteria erupted. Once again, in their excitement, they drowned out the rest of the rap. San-Man winked at me. I stepped into the circle and just as he passed the mic to me, the school bell rang.

*"I'm MC Shry...,"* I began. But it was too late. The crowd was shuffling off to their next class. I had missed my big break.

But in hindsight, it was a good thing—I was so nervous that instead of spittin' fresh rhymes, I might have vomited. But soon I would have my chance to shine, on one of the biggest stages in the history of Lake Charles.

**M**Y YOUNG LIFE BEGAN TO FEEL LIKE ONE LONG BOUT OF performance anxiety. I'd get *this close* to tasting success only to find out that God had somehow tricked me into gulping a tablespoon of liquid Ex-Lax.

That year saw the first of what would become a frequent occurrence in my life. I dubbed it the celebrity scenario. Every few years, I would find myself in an unusual situation involving a celebrity.

One Sunday afternoon, Andre and I were driving home from church services. We had just left a citywide youth revival meeting. Andre had finally coaxed me into going to the function—it was something he had been going to for years. I soon found out why. The meeting was a precursor to the annual Baptist Youth Encampment, five days of Bible classes, gospel concerts, and Christian fellowshipping among teenagers throughout the state. Baptist Youth Encampment or Camp, as regulars called it, was also five days of getting your freak on.

Held the first week in August on the campus of Southern University in Baton Rouge, Camp attracted nearly 2,000 teenagers between the ages of fifteen and nineteen from all over Louisiana, Texas, and even as far away as Florida. The campers were split up into Boys Town and Girls Town, and were housed in student dormitories. There were 1,200 girls compared to 600-plus guys, and out of those it seemed half had to be gay. Another hundred or so were still scared talk to girls. So, that left about 200 horny boys to be split up between more than a thousand young, nubile girls. Although I was Baptist, I thought we had died and gone to Muslim heaven, where they reward you with seventy-two virgins for every man. It was that lopsided ratio that convinced a young demon like myself to join a church in the first place. See, you couldn't attend Camp if you weren't a baptized member of a church. In essence, I got saved so that I could sin.

So there Andre and I were, on our way home discussing what new outfits we were going to wear to church camp, when I motioned him toward a Burger King on Martin Luther King Highway near our home on Guinn Street. Andre dropped me off and as I walked across the parking lot, I noticed a group of about six or seven guys standing around the drive-through window.

As I got closer, I saw what the commotion was about. The commotion's name was Bonita Prejean, a very attractive high-yella-looking model-type who attended Washington Marion. Bonita, who looked like Pocahontas, manned the drive-through window at Burger King.

"What time you get off?" I overheard one of the guys ask her.

Another guy pushed him out the way then asked, "You got any friends that look like you?"

Bonita slammed the drive-through window shut. In their sheepskin vests, spiked wristbands, stonewashed blue jeans, and leather boots, the guys looked like Jheri-curled gangbangers. They definitely weren't from Lake Charles—nobody in our town dressed like that. I avoided eye contact and kept walking. One of the guys noticed me and headed over.

"Yo, my man, hold up," he said.

*Damn,* I thought, but kept on walking. I had no desire to get jumped by a group of out-of-towners. I just wanted a Whopper.

But the guy was persistent. "Wait up, brother. You know where I can get some weed?"

I sped up the pace. The door was in sight. "Nah, man, I don't know nothing about no weed." In truth, I had a bag the size of Shaquille O'Neal in my pocket.

"Yo, it's cool. I ain't no cop," he whispered. "I'm with Grandmaster Flash and the Furious Five."

I stopped dead in my tracks and smacked my lips. "Grandmaster Flash my ass."

He laughed and handed me a flyer with the group's photo on it. "See, that's me. I'm Rahiem. We're here from New York for the Fresh Fest."

*Of course,* I thought. The New York City Fresh Fest Tour was in town

ONCE AGAIN, FORTUNE WAS SMILING ON ME, BUT WAS I TOO nearsighted to see how crooked her teeth were. Riding high on the excitement of being associated with famous rap stars, I was convinced that I too was destined to become famous. I also wanted all of Lake Charles to realize this. My group and I would have the chance to prove it at a big local talent show called The Showcase, to be held at Washington Marion. It was home turf and we would have hundreds of supporters.

"We gon' kill 'em," Bubba sneered.

*Well, not literally,* I thought, while eyeing SupaThug.

The Showcase had people from all of the area high schools signing up. All types of acts, from rappers to dance groups to singers, would be on the bill. Armed with a cheap Casio drum machine, the Lake City Boys began writing songs and rehearsing in my garage. While San-Man and I sat on some old tires, Bubba laid down a hot drumbeat on the Casio, then beat boxed over it. As usual, Miny Mo just stood off to the side silent. Soon, the rhythmic track had us nodding like heroin addicts.

*"Rehearsal? Rehearsal?"* San-Man freestyled. *"My style is Universal."*

*"It's The Real Thing/Like on them Coke commercials."*

San-Man stopped, an unsure look on his face. "How's that sound?"

"I like that, I like that," I smiled. "After you say commercial, I'ma come in like,"

*"Holy Smokes!/I energize the crowd like Coke."*

*"I'm no joke/I'm known worldwide like the Pope."*

San-man jumped up. "Wait, wait, I got something that can go with that."

*"Before I quote/I rinse my mouth out with Scope."*
*"So that my notes/Can fly free from my throat."*

I had a smile on my face that would have made Buckwheat jealous. I didn't have to say a word. I just gave San-Man a pound.

"Y'all like Batman and Robin," Bubba joked.

But the night of The Showcase, we felt more like Abbott and Costello. Outside the gym in the parking lot, we sat smoking weed inside the Green Hornet, Bubba's beat-up 1978 Pontiac Bonneville Classic. We watched nervously as a steady stream of students made their way inside the gym.

"Must be a thousand people in there," Miny Mo calculated.

Bubba coughed and nodded in agreement as he passed a banana-sized joint to San-Man. While he puffed, I reached over from the backseat for the forty-ounce bottle of Old English 800 Bubba was nursing.

"Let me get a swig of that."

I turned the bottle up and gulped it like Gatorade. I needed to calm my nerves. I had pterodactyls flapping around inside my stomach.

The Lake City Boys were the second act on the bill, but it was clear from the first note uttered by the first act, a gospel singer, that the road to the title wouldn't be a cakewalk. To make it worse, the gospel singer was a *very* cute little black girl, maybe ten or eleven. To make it *worser,* she had an angelic smile to go along with those little Shirley Temple curls. To make it the *worst,* she sang "Amazing Grace." A cappella. And killed it.

"I could just hug her," someone in the audience yelled. Meanwhile, I wanted to slap her.

By the time that little girl finished, I knew we were finished. But SupaThug wasn't going down without a fight. From backstage we could hear the MC announce our name. Then the familiar groove of our song started playing on the loudspeakers.

"I ain't losing to no little-ass girl," Bubba promised. "Watch this."

To our astonishment, Bubba pulled out a pistol and started firing at the ceiling as he walked on stage first.

"What the…?" I flinched, looking at San-Man, who was just as surprised as I was. It was only a starter's pistol but people were ducking and running for cover like they were about to get robbed. And the way Bubba was acting, I wasn't so sure they weren't.

"Okay, motherfuckers, it's a stick-up," Bubba yelled into the microphone.

"That boy is crazy," Miny Mo laughed. San-Man and I just shook our heads. Once the audience realized they weren't about to get shot, they went bananas. One by one Bubba introduced us. He, San-Man, and I had on long tan overcoats, while Miny Mo was looking dapper in a tan suit with a matching tie and handkerchief. The crowd went berserk when we walked— or rather staggered—on stage. We were drunker than that crazy uncle you avoid at family reunions.

"It Show----time," I slurred.

San-Man winked at me and began rhyming.

*I'm the S-A-N Dash M-A-N.*

We had the crowd in the palms of our hands. The way they were going nuts, there was no way that we could lose. Well, maybe one way. As San-Man was tossing to me, the sound system went haywire. It sounded like our tape was being eaten alive. The noise was overwhelming. I was rapping my heart out, but all that was coming from the speakers was garbled static. I froze. Then the crowd sat frozen in silence. Miny Mo walked off the stage.

We looked at the MC. He shrugged his shoulders as if to say, "What you looking at me for?"

Then Bubba, bless his heart, started beat-boxing, but that made it worse.

That's when the crowd started to boo. It started as a low rumble, but seconds later the boos and jeers had become deafening. They even threw things at the stage. I was mortified. It was like bombing at Harlem's fabled Apollo.

*Why are they doing this?* I stood there wondering. *It's not our fault.*

But the sharks were circling and didn't care who was at fault. All they smelled was blood in the water. Who can really resist a good boo? Dejected, we shuffled off stage like we were shackled at the ankles. The Lake City Boys were dead. Backstage, Greg "Hollywood" Henderson attempted to cheer us up.

"Y'all looked like asses out there," he said.

As I leaned against the wall half-listening to Greg diss us, I imagined ways to kill myself. Can a person really be embarrassed to death? I wanted a simple headstone with the inscription, "Byron, finished at sixteen."

Since it was Thursday night, we still had to go to school the next day. Knowing that we were going to get crucified, we agreed as a group to stick together and show up for class. The next day, however, I was the only one to show up for school. Although I wore one of my best outfits, as I walked the halls on my way to homeroom I couldn't hide my "I'm embarrassed" face. There is just no way to control your facial muscles when you are that embarrassed. As I passed one group of girls, I could overhear one of them whisper that we were "wack." I tried my best to ignore it, but it hurt me to the core. Everywhere I turned, students snickered or turned their heads away. I felt like I had gotten caught masturbating.

I T WAS AROUND THE TIME OF OUR TALENT SHOW FLAME-OUT THAT I stumbled upon a mantra from *Unlimited Power,* a book by Anthony Robbins, the famous motivational speaker, that I would carry with me for the rest of my life. It went something like this:

*There is no such thing as failure, only undesired results.*

I said it again, this time aloud. *"There is no such thing as failure, only undesired results."*

The concept hit me like a left hook to the chin. Basically, it took the failing out of failure. The key is that you make the attempt. Too often, people never truly realize their full potential because they are afraid of failing. If the outcome is less than desirable, step back and assess where you went wrong, then try again. I have since found great joy in the adventure and pursuit of a goal, no matter the outcome. At the risk of sounding like a televangelist, I felt like God had whispered in my ear. In God's breath came the whisper of wisdom.

*"There is no such thing as failure, only undesired results."*

I loved that phrase. It sounded to me like secret knowledge found in dusty long hidden manuscripts of wizards, stuff ordinary humans weren't meant to hear. All I had to do was convince myself that it was true. My tiny bedroom looking out on Guinn Street became my laboratory. It was where I would create my own new man—me. I began a long, slow process of self-examination, focused particularly on all the times that I'd failed or quit at something. While it was true that the results were definitely undesired, the moments still stank with the pungent aroma of failure. Soon, I discovered that I wasn't really quitting teams or jobs or things—I was quitting on myself.

*There is no such thing as failure, only undesired results.*

I repeated it over and over until slowly, the meaning of it began to transform my outlook on life. From then on, I was waging war with rifles while my fellow students were yanking on slingshots.

However, by the end of my junior year at Washington Marion, I found out that there certainly is such a thing as failure, if you were looking at my GPA.

By that time, though, I had no practical use for public school any more. How could I? I didn't have the time. Lake Charles might as well have been Las Vegas, as far as I was concerned, I was rolling the dice nearly every night. There were so many places to party.

Sunday nights you'd catch me at Skate City roller rink. Hundreds of kids from all over Lake Charles would be in there skating. But real players didn't skate—or, as in my case, they couldn't. I'd been embarrassed enough in my young life without risking spinal injury trying to impress some girl with a deft spin move. So my crew and I would be outside, "parking lot pimping" and smoking weed until 9 pm, when the skating ended and the dancing began.

You had to roll deep at the rink. Fights were de rigueur, so it was a must to have reliable backup. My crew normally consisted of Bubba (who drove), Craig, and Miny Mo. We also hung out with a couple of cool thugs who were also Bubba's cousins, who attended our cross-town rival, Lake Charles Boston High School. I want to stress that I was never a thug in any way, shape, or form. I just happened to have a bunch of friends who were. I have always had the gift of blending in and out of any social group with ease. Throughout the course of a day at school, I'd be in advanced chemistry class with the nerds, then between classes I'd spit a little original poetry to the artistic cliques. Later on, I'd hang out and smoke weed and drink beer with the jocks at lunchtime, but still could roll out to parties with the boys in the hood. I never tried to act tough, and I never got into any major fights, since it was hard to fight in some of the outfits I wore.

By this time I was wearing what could only be described as some outrageously strange shit. I'm very conservative in my dress now, but back then I thought nothing of sporting a gray half-cut waiter jacket with matching pants, a light gray wing-tipped shirt, a gray and red striped leather tie, and (the piece de resistance) a pair of gleaming red Stacy Adams shoes.

Yes, red shoes. I am not ashamed. You know how many phone numbers

I got because of those red shoes? I had some pink ones, too, but I only wore them on special occasions. Hey, the male peacock with the brightest feathers is the one who gets to mate, right?

After the skating rink closed at midnight, the party moved to Taco Bell on Highway 171. In front of the restaurant was a strip of pavement on which drunken kids waved from the sunroofs of souped-up cars slowly driving by, blasting rap cranked up to ear splitting levels. Taco Bell was the hot after-spot—that is, until a friend of mine named Kevin Mayo, a legendary local pugilist, beat the hell out of two guys in a drunken rage, and then for extra effect ripped down an entire wooden fence separating Taco Bell from the Calcasieu State Bank.

Those were Sunday nights. Sunday afternoons were reserved for the Civic Center and the Lake. The Civic Center was a huge complex right off the lake where all of the major concerts were held. Thousands of young people would gather there to hang out and profile—that is, until Washington Marion went to war with Lagrange High School and some kids got stomped half to death there. The Civic Center had hosted plenty of events but never a heavyweight fight.

That was my first exposure to Kevin Mayo's equally legendary cousin, Roman Thompson, who would later become my brother Andre's best friend and an honorary member of our family. Roman attended Lagrange, a school we considered soft because it had white students (I can only remember Washington Marion having one white student, Darrel Bouillion, but his family was as broke as any of ours, so he fit right in). Roman—6'4", and built like a linebacker—was far from soft. That fateful afternoon at the Civic Center, I witnessed him beat up four hard-asses from Washington Marion. Knocked one guy right out of his sneakers. Roman was funny, and blessed with charisma worthy of a presidential candidate or a boxing promoter.

Tuesdays meant dollar movie nights at the Oak Park Cinema. I saw *Star Wars*, *Jaws*, *Krush Groove*, and *The Last Dragon* there. I only *saw* them, however, because you couldn't *hear* anything, not with the theater packed to the rafters with hooligans like myself laughing, talking, and even smoking. We smuggled Popeye's Chicken and forty-ounce bottles of Colt .45 into the theater to sip with our popcorn. Dollar nights were great fun—that is, until people started getting shot in the parking lot.

I couldn't wait for Saturday nights, when we used to party at Club Fantastic's on Broad Street. I was only sixteen, but I could pass for twenty-three, and never had a problem getting in as long as I didn't try to drink inside the club. That was okay, because I drank plenty outside the club. Club Fantastic's was the place to be—that is, until hot lead rained in the parking lot and a couple of people got "wet."

The list of grand openings and closings was a long one. The famous Doll House on Mill Street? Shot up and shut down numerous times. Jones's Fine Fox on Highway 171? Enter at your own risk. The Figure 8 on the infamously violent Enterprise Boulevard? The Figure 8 got eighty-sixed in a devastating fire.

It was the dawn of the crack era, and people in Lake Charles were trading in their bongs for pipes. It was the time when my thug friends stopped fighting with their fists and started living—and dying—by the gun. Even I was spiraling out of control. In a blind jealous rage, I nearly stabbed a student named Wilray Victorian outside a classroom after I learned that he was calling a girl I was dating. Okay, he was screwing a girl that I had been dating. I had every intention of cutting his heart out. Bubba saved Wilray's life, and possibly mine, too, by wrestling my knife away from me and running off with it before one of our coaches (who doubled as school security) busted up our fight.

The following week, Bubba, Miny Mo, and myself were busted with half a pound of marijuana and a case of Old English 800. Needless to say, I was scared shitless—especially after we realized we were being busted by Officer Kowalski, a notoriously mean and brutal city cop. He lined us up against Bubba's car and roughly frisked us. He refused to believe we were sixteen since he was already well acquainted with Bubba, who was nearly eighteen. Bubba didn't have his license or registration, his tags were expired, he was without insurance, and he was under the influence. Officer Kowalski nearly choked Miny Mo, who had a full beard and a voice that sounded like a forty-year-old chain smoker's. I knew my father would not bail me out, and would probably disown me. I sent out an instant S.O.S to God. Incredibly, Officer Kowalski confiscated our weed and made us pour all of our beer out on the ground, and then let us go with a sneer and a warning.

A couple of weeks later Bubba got into an argument with his cousin Hilton. When Hilton pulled out a .22, Bubba just laughed at the little-bitty gun and dared him to shoot. It was a dare Bubba lost. Hilton blasted Bubba in the foot. Hilton then waved the gun in our direction and asked if we wanted any. We didn't.

It was against this backdrop of partying and bullet-dodging that school became a waste of time for me. Thank God I had only one more year left on my sentence—or so I thought.

We arrived at school early on the day they gave out our final report cards. I was with Bubba, Craig Joseph, and Miny Mo, and we were in a hurry. There was a big party, an annual end-of-school shindig, being held at the beach by the lake. It wasn't really a beach, but a man-made sandy patch of land. We called it the Bleach. The brackish, muddy Bleach was surrounded by a handful of petrochemical plants, so only fools rushed into the water. But the end-of-school party was always a spectacular affair. This party was going to be special because we would now be seniors and could officially act a damn fool. Our motto was going to be "All the way to heaven in '87," after the song by Doug E. Fresh.

By the time we made it to Washington Marion, I thought it was Mardi Gras. The hallways were raucous with smiling soon-to-be seniors dancing and waving their report cards in the air chanting, "All the way to heaven in '87." I couldn't wait to join in the conga line. The guys and I split up and raced to our separate homerooms. We planned to meet up shortly at Bubba's car to start celebrating.

The mood inside and outside my homeroom was festive. It was like everybody had hit the jackpot. Well, almost everybody. I should have known something was fishy when Mrs. St. John, my always-chipper teacher, avoided eye contact as she handed me my report card.

I smiled before doing an about-face. I didn't bother to even *glance* at my report card. What for? With the gimme classes I was taking, I knew I had passed. I continued on through the hallways stopping every now and then to hug a female classmate or to slap the back of a fellow new senior.

"All the way to heaven in '87," I said.

"Back at 'cha, B.H.," they chanted.

In the parking lot, the volume knobs on the car stereos were twisted to the maximum. Guys were ogling some of more free-spirited young ladies who were dancing provocatively.

That's when I ran into Tammy Diamond, one of the finest specimens of the female form to have ever been specified. I, along with a quite a few of my male fellow students, had fantasized about Tammy ever since she was in the sixth grade. I couldn't pass up an opportunity to cop a free feel. Tammy reached out and hugged me.

"See you at the Bleach," I smiled, after hungrily running my fingers up and down her back.

In the heat of my lust, I dropped my report card on the ground. I bent down to pick it up and what I saw still haunts me. The card was stamped with the word "RETAINED."

Retained? I thought, while pints of blood rushed to my head. What a strange way to spell PASSED. Maybe it was Latin?

I became dizzy and breathless. I tried to swallow but my throat was too dry. My knees were weak and my teeth clicked together. I was sure that I was on the verge of a stroke. Everyone and everything around me started moving in slow motion.

"All the wayyyy tooooo heeeavennnnn," my friends chanted, but to me their voices were mocking, distorted, and warped.

Bubba shook me out of my stupor. "C'mon B.H., let's go. We seniors now. All the way to heaven in '87, baaaaaby!"

I smiled weakly and half-heartedly pumped my fist. "Yeah… All…. the…way…to…heaven."

I quickly stuffed the report card in my pocket. I went into a sort of zone. It would be my first experience with a technique I gradually developed that enables me to block out my surroundings and calmly focus on the problem at hand. My mind raced for a solution. What could I do? I was sure of only one thing—there was no way I was repeating the eleventh grade, at least not at Washington Marion. That would be the ultimate indignity. I would join the Peace Corps and move to Sierra Leone before I'd do that.

All of my other misbehaviors to this point were minor. I shook them off with no problems, but being held back a grade? This would be my Watergate. My Waterloo. I'd be disgraced. Something had to be done, and fast. I had a beach party to get to.

While walking behind Bubba, I eased the card back out of my pocket and scanned it for clues. I actually had decent grades that year, so I was baffled. Then my eyes fixed on my Spanish grade. F?

I was so mad I bit my bottom lip. Must be a mistake. Hell, I *hablo'd* with the best of them.

"Bubba, I'll meet ya'll at the beach. I gotta take care of something," I said before running off.

"Yo," he yelled after me but I had *adios*'ed.

I was out of breath when I got to Ms. Rodriguez's classroom. She was my Spanish teacher and she was all business.

"Ms. Rodriguez," I smiled. "There must be some mistake. My report card has me failing your class."

Ms. Rodriguez looked up from her desk. She casually removed the pair of Mrs. Crabtree glasses that were perched on the tip of her nose. "There was no mistake, Mr. Harmon. I indeed failed you."

My jaw fell to the floor with a thud. "But I had all As and Bs each grading period."

"Except for the last one—you missed a lot of days," she explained with the coolness of a judge ruling on a misdemeanor.

I sucked my teeth in amazement. "But I had an operation in March, remember? The absences were excused." I really did have an operation, a minor one to lance a boil. I had been out of school for two weeks.

Ms. Rodriguez was nonplussed. "What about your homework assignments you failed to turn in?"

My face became a blank sheet of paper, and on it was written the word *gotcha*. "Uh, well," I coughed, clearing a nonexistent obstruction in my throat. "You see, what happened was..."

She waved me off. "What happened was, you blew off your responsibilities, young man. Well, Mr. Harmon, there are consequences for blowing off your responsibilities."

I wanted to blow her head off, but I begged instead. "Aw, c'mon, Ms. Rodriguez, I need this class to be a senior."

She shrugged her shoulders.

I blew my stack. "This is Louisiana, not fuckin' Spain. Why in the hell I need to know this shit anyway?" I said before storming out of the classroom. "I don't even like Mexican food."

Now what to do? As I aimlessly walked the hallways, I wondered how old I needed to be in order to join the Merchant Marines. That's when I saw Roscoe Moore, the principal, and an idea hit me like a bolt of lightning.

Ever since I had quit football at the end of my sophomore year, Roscoe had been aggressively recruiting me to come back and play. I had no interest in it, and I avoided him like a broke relative. But I was desperate. So I walked right up to Roscoe and lied like a police informant.

"Mr. Moore, I'm ready to play football," I said.

He grinned a toothy smile. "That's good, boy. Glad to hear it."

I frowned and sorrowfully gazed away at the floor. "But I got one problem, sir."

"Nonsense," he bellowed. "We don't have problems, only solutions."

I then went on to explain that Ms. Rodriguez had failed me, and why. And that my father would not allow me to play football if I had failed. Roscoe slapped me on my back and agreed that it was a tragic miscarriage of justice. "Come with me to my office," he said.

"Gladly," I smiled.

He changed my grade right then and there. I was so happy I felt like I had hit the lottery, but I hedged my bet just in case Roscoe tried the "ole okey-doke" later on. I had my mother come to school to confirm that I was going "all the way to heaven…in '87."

At the Bleach, I partied like a sailor on a weekend pass. It was official, I was now a senior—but one with strings attached. But as Roscoe would find out soon enough, I had no plans to have any of my strings pulled on the football field.

OUR SENIOR YEAR STARTED OFF NOT WITH A BANG BUT A BLAZE. One morning while watching the local news and getting ready for school, I watched Washington Marion go up in flames.

"I'm standing outside Washington Marion," the cute TV reporter announced as sirens flashed and smoke swirled in the background, "where officials say the fire apparently started in one of the air conditioning units. Arson is suspected." Finally, we had earned the letter "a" in K-MART.

Moments later the phone rang. It was Bubba. "You watching TV?"

"I can't believe it," I said.

"I'm coming to scoop you up," Bubba said, and then hung up. The phone kept ringing, and each time it was a buddy expressing shock.

Bubba came to get me, and then we swung around to pick up Craig before heading to school, but not before committing some arson of our own on the unlit end of a joint. When we arrived at school, we witnessed a mob of students chanting in front of the fire trucks.

"The roof, the roof, the roof is on fire," they roared with gusto. "We don't need no water, let the motherfucker burn! Burn, motherfucker, burn!" My classmates had given the phrase "torch song" a new meaning.

While they sang, others hoped to fan the flames by praying for a nice stiff breeze. Their prayers fell on deaf ears, since most of the school escaped major damage. However, many classrooms were uninhabitable, forcing school officials to partition the girls' gym into a series of tiny plywood-walled classrooms.

The question on everyone's lips was, "Whodunit?" It didn't take long

73

to find out there was no more honor amongst arsonists than there is among thieves. Cops caught one of the culprits the very next day. Word on the street had him bragging about the job all over town. Under questioning, the guy sang louder than the Harlem Boys Choir. The other two members of his crew were soon rounded up. All were seniors, like me—and shockingly, one of them was the son of a school secretary.

The fire and its aftermath kept Roscoe Moore so occupied he barely noticed that I had not once been to football practice. In fact, I had not even approached the coach about playing. I played my dangerous game of cat and mouse for nearly a month before Roscoe cornered me by the cafeteria. He looked at me the way a loan shark eyes a chronic late payer.

"Hey boy, why ain't yo' ass playin' ball?"

As was my custom under intense questioning, I cleared my throat. "I uh, it's that operation I had sir, I can barely even bend."

It was a weak sell, and Roscoe wasn't buying. He waved a long bony finger and warned, "I'ma remember you." Then he walked off, probably to go harass some other student.

I feared that Roscoe might reverse my passing grade, thus blocking my eventual graduation. Roscoe had a bit of a Don King quality to his personality, so I wasn't entirely sure of what to expect. For the rest of the year, the specter of not graduating floated in the air.

The brightest spot of my senior year was that I only had to go to class for half a day. Since I worked at Piccadilly, I qualified for a program that enabled students to earn school credit for working. According to the rules, students had to work after school, but I had long since switched my work schedule from weekdays to weekends. That way, I was able to work the same amount of hours in just two days, giving me more free time during the week. My manager wasn't aware of the rules and just blindly signed off on the paperwork. I was back in bed every day by noon.

The DECA instructor was named Mrs. Jones. She was in her mid- to late thirties, but her body was still stuck in her late teens. Mrs. Jones was a snake charmer, and when she held court in front of the class, I was like a cobra moving back and forth with the swaying of her curvy hips. Word on the street was that at one time or another, Mrs. Jones had dated a lucky boy or two, and the way in which she looked at me made me feel very lucky myself.

I got my chance during the 1987 Super Bowl. The New York Giants were playing the Denver Broncos. Mrs. Jones was an avid sports fan, and one day after class, as I helped "dust the erasers," we made a friendly wager on the game.

"What's the bet?" she asked.

I smiled mischievously. "If Denver wins, you take me out to dinner."

She nodded her head. "Okay. If New York wins, you take me out to dinner."

It took a moment for me to realize that I couldn't lose.

The day of the Super Bowl, the Giants beat Denver 39 to 20. I owed Mrs. Jones a date, and I was a young man who always paid his debts. For two weeks I played Billy Paul's "Me and Mrs. Jones" on my old raggedy record player. The night she picked me up felt like prom night.

"Who's that lady outside?" my mother asked.

"My teacher," I said, walking out the door.

I heard my mother ask, "How old is that woman?"

I had decided to take Mrs. Jones to a nice French restaurant, but really, the only French I was interested in was French kissing. As the night went on, we laughed and had great conversation, but I was too stupid to realize that I was out of my league. She threw me softballs but I repeatedly kept fouling them off.

"You know, Byron," she whispered while seductively biting her lower lip, "My husband doesn't give me any attention or affection. All he cares about is watching television."

"Maybe he's tired," I suggested between mouthfuls of crawfish étouffée.

She switched tactics after we finished dessert. While making herself more comfortable in her seat, her ample breasts did their best to break free from her lace blouse.

"So Byron, what do you want to do now?" she purred.

I rubbed my chin in thought. "I guess you can drop me home."

I didn't notice Mrs. Jones rolling her eyes. "Uh, okay."

She lobbed one last pitch as we sat in my driveway. "So when are *you* going to pick *me* up?"

"I don't really know," I admitted. "My father has revoked my driving privileges for the moment."

There it was—I had finally struck out. Our relationship was never the same after that night. From then on, she began to treat me like just another student.

All I had to look forward to after that fiasco was graduating. It was the biggest event of the year, but because I had broken my promise to play football, I wasn't sure that I'd get a ticket.

*Not graduating?* The thought had been lodged in the back of my mind all year long. I took graduation pictures, bought invitations, and did the whole bit, but I never was completely sure that I really would graduate. The icy way Roscoe would look at me when I ran into him did little to allay my fears. My not graduating would top any and all lists of the most embarrassing things that could ever happen to me. Along with my classmates, I got measured for my cap and gown. It felt more like I was getting fitted for a funeral shroud.

The weeks dragged on and graduation drew near. While nearly all the seniors knew they were graduating, a handful were in situations similar to mine. I found out the official list of graduates wouldn't be posted until three days before graduation.

My one saving grace had been my grades that year. With half-day classes and the rest of my class schedule consisting of advanced finger painting and music appreciation, I knew I had the grades. Roscoe held the wildcard and he was playing it close to the vest.

The day of the posting, I approached the bulletin board like it was a tranquilized lion. I cautiously fingered the names. Handy, Haney, Hardy, Harmon. I blinked hard. Yep, there I was.

I pumped my fist in the air. It was a good thing too, since I had already spent all my graduation gift money.

**B**AM, BAM, BAM, THE DOOR OF MY BEDROOM BANGED. OF COURSE, it was Pops. "Get ya ass up. It ain't your birthday."

The morning after graduation, Pops dragged me out of bed and sat me down at the dinner table to go over my options.

"Do we have to do this at six o'clock in the morning?" I asked, bleary-eyed. My previous night's debauchery would have made Caligula squeamish. Pops was very familiar with hangovers and poured me a steaming cup of coffee.

"Son, you got two choices," he explained, casually sipping from his favorite mug. "You can join the military. You can go to jail. But here's one thing about which you have no choice: you are getting the hell out of my house."

That afternoon I ate chow with an Army recruiter. I was so nervous that my knees were shaking when I arrived at the recruiting station. Outside there were Vegas-like neon signs blinking out the words "Army," "Navy," "Air Force," and "Marines." Representatives from each branch stood at various styles of attention by each door. I looked at the Navy guy.

"Hi, sailor," he smiled, a bit too seductively.

*Oh hell no*, I thought, shaking my head. There wasn't any way I was going on a ship out in the ocean for six months with a bunch of dudes. I had no interest in becoming a *rear* admiral.

Next was the Air Force guy. He looked very relaxed and by the size of his belly, extremely well fed, but the waiting list was more than a year. *Pops will kill me by then*, I thought, and shuffled along.

77

The hulking Marine was well over six feet tall and so fit that even his lips had muscles. His eyes were dead and empty. "You want to be a killer?" he asked.

*I want my mommy*, I thought, flinching before giving him a wide berth on my way into the Army office.

A short, pudgy sergeant greeted me with a weak handshake.

*I guess they don't exercise anymore in the Army*, I thought. *Sign me up.*

The sergeant gave me the standard "Be all you can be" stuff about serving your country. I bet that he could've recited the spiel in his sleep. To him, I was a quota number.

"What type of job are you interested in?" he inquired.

I smiled—that was an easy one. "The type of job that has the least amount of work." Sarge didn't get the joke. "Something behind a desk," I explained. "I want to be a 71 Lima and be stationed at Fort Benjamin Harrison."

The recruiter raised an eyebrow, impressed with my knowledge of Army nomenclature. This was a recruit he couldn't trick. Seventy-one Lima was the official MOS designation for a personnel specialist. A friend of mine had hipped me to it, and told me that Fort Benjamin Harrison, located in Indianapolis, was crawling with women of questionable morals.

"How long you want to sign up for?" The recruiter asked.

I casually held up two fingers.

He typed "two years" and "Fort Benjamin Harrison" into his computer. Looking at all the action posters hanging on the wall, I started daydreaming about all the fine sisters I'd be meeting and, with that tax-free money, how I would finally be able to afford them. A few moments later, the recruiter sighed heavily.

I straightened in the chair. "What's wrong?"

There was a look of disappointment on his face. "We got a problem. Seems there are no more slots left for 71 Limas."

"Oh well, too bad," I stood, looking for the nearest exit.

The recruiter reached for my arm. "Wait, lemme see what I can do." He began furiously pecking away at the keyboard. A few moments later he said, "Byron, my man, it's your lucky day."

I rubbed my hands together excitedly. "You found a slot?"

He shook his head. "No, I had to pull some strings, but I found you something even better."

*Even better?* It was my turn to raise an eyebrow. *I didn't know the Army had an opening for a gigolo,* I thought. *Because that's the only job that could be better than a cushy desk job surrounded by lots of women.*

"What is it?" I asked, cautiously.

The sergeant leaned back in his chair, rubbed his belly, and smiled like a used car salesman. "13 Foxtrot. Fire Support Specialist."

A look of confusion crossed my cherubic face. "A fireman?"

"No," he laughed before scrounging around on his desk for a laserdisc. "Watch this. It'll blow your mind."

For the next five minutes I saw the most exciting and eye-catching recruiting commercial ever. The Army must have hired Steven Spielberg to film the spot. There were bombs blowing up all over the place, soldiers running around firing M16s and driving Hummers at breakneck speeds, not to mention the jets and helicopters buzzing by. Not once did I see anybody wash a pot. I sat there with my mouth hanging open like a hounddog. The recruiter placed a crisp new contract on his desk and looked at me like he was offering me a major record deal. "That, my friend, is a fire support specialist."

"Where do I sign?"

The recruiter had a devilish smile and passed me a thick stack of forms. After signing what seemed like a thousand sheets of paper, I called Pops and told him the good news about my new job. After the past few years of screwing up, I knew he'd be proud.

"You chose what? Thirteen Foxtrot, for three years? Why did you do something stupid like that?" he barked before hanging up the phone. Jeez, I couldn't win.

By that time my relationship with Pops had deteriorated to a point where it seemed irreparable. That long hot summer we barely spoke to each other. As we'd pass each other in the hallway, we'd eye each other like Ali and Joe Frazier. My mother was the referee.

"Dave, leave that boy alone," she'd say.

He would stare at her with ice cubes in his eyes. "This is my damn house. I pay the bills around here."

I wasn't due to ship off to Basic Training until September, so I had the whole summer left to piss off Pops. I went totally off the deep end. One weekend Andre and I snuck out of the house and flew to Tampa, Florida. Some girls we had met at Baptist Youth Encampment bought us some round-trip tickets. We barely knew these girls and had no business going to Florida. Pops was dead set against it.

"If y'all go to Florida, don't come back," he snapped.

Dre and I looked at each other and telepathically communicated.

*Screw that. We're going to Florida.*

We almost didn't come back from Florida. What we didn't know was that the girls had boyfriends who didn't take too kindly to some slick country boys from Louisiana coming to see their women. Under the pretense of inviting us to a party, they tried to lure us to the Ponce de Leon housing projects, a notoriously violent section of Tampa. The girls warned us we'd better get the hell out of town or risk a case of severe lead poisoning.

We flew back to New Orleans and decided to stay a few days and see some friends. One thing led to another, and three days later I woke up from a drunken stupor to find myself in Baton Rouge, in the apartment of a beautiful Southern University dancing doll. By the time Andre and I made it back to Lake Charles, we were drained and flat broke. I just wanted to sleep. I couldn't wait to get in my own bed. When we arrived at the house, our keys didn't work. Pops had changed the locks.

"Open up the door," I lightly tapped on the window. I could see Pops sitting in his recliner watching a Western. He ignored me.

"Aw c'mon, quit tripping," I pleaded.

My mother came to the door and pulled back the curtain. It pained her to see her two oldest boys locked out in the humid night. My brother Marshall, seven years younger than me, was in our bedroom playing Nintendo.

"Don't you open that door," Pops warned.

"Dave, let them boys in."

He casually turned his attention back to the Western and turned up the volume on the television's remote control.

I blew my top. "That's okay!" I yelled. "I'm leaving for the Army in three weeks and I ain't never coming back here."

Andre grabbed my arm, attempting to calm me down. But I was a man possessed.

"You hear me? I ain't never coming back. Y'all make me sick."

My mother was on the verge of tears, but Pops was unmoved.

"Bye," he waved. "One less mouth to feed."

Damn, Pops was cold. One time, in a typical fit of teenaged angst I had threatened to blow my brains out. He didn't even look up from the newspaper. "Can you do it in the backyard so you won't mess up my carpet?" he asked.

My mother eventually calmed my father down and let us in. I walked
by Pops without making eye contact. My impending departure was making
my mother a little softer. On the morning I left for Basic Training, you
would have thought I was going off to fight World War II. She even let me
sleep in.

"Here's something to eat," she fussed over me. "Don't forget to call
when you get there. You got some pajamas?"

Pops frowned. "Shirley, the boy is going to boot camp, not a slumber
party."

As the big day neared, even Pops loosened the reins. He even let me
borrow his prized van for my last weekend as a civilian.

"I don't want you drinking, and I definitely don't want none of your
trifling-ass friends in my van," he said, tentatively handing me the keys.

"Of course, Pops." I thanked him before picking up some of my trifling
friends and stopping off at Smitty's on Moeling Street, one of many liquor
stores that openly sold alcohol to minors.

I forgot what we did, but I assume it must have otherwise been a night
to remember. The next morning, Pops was banging on my bedroom door
like he was SWAT. I bolted upright in the bed yawning, wiping the cold
from my eyes.

"Didn't I tell you not to be drinking and driving in my damn van?"
he yelled. A long throbbing thick vein creased his forehead. "I should kick
your ass."

I quickly ran through the night in my mind. I didn't wreck the van,
didn't get any tickets, plus I'd cleaned it thoroughly of any contraband.

I shrugged, feigning innocence. "What are you talking 'bout, Pops?"

He stormed over the window and jerked open the curtains. "Look
outside."

I shook my head in disbelief. I had parked my father's van right in the
middle of our front yard.

That was the last straw. Pops told me he couldn't wait for me to leave.
He was silent as he helped load my bags for the drive to the bus station.
As we pulled out of the driveway, my mother with tears in her eyes waved
goodbye. I will never, ever forget that sight. Up until that moment, I had
been a rock but when I saw my *momma* crying, my eyes couldn't help
but well up. I wanted to run back into the house, hug her, and wash the
dishes, cut the grass, or rake the leaves one last time. Anything but leave my
momma and go to the Army.

The ride to the Greyhound station was tortuous. Pops seemed to be driving in slow motion. I tried to savor every sight, every sound, and every smell of Guinn Street. I weakly waved at my neighbors going about their everyday routines. Most of my friends were going to college or had landed jobs at one of the chemical plants. I was the only dummy who was joining the Army. As we passed by Nelson and Craig's house, there was a huge basketball game in progress. Their yard looked like a street festival and everybody was having fun—too much fun, the most fun ever. That tore me up inside. I thought of how most of them had laughed and said I was crazy for joining the Army. I turned my head to avoid making eye contact with anyone.

*What was I getting myself into?*

No doubt about it. I was scared. I prayed to God that I was making the right decision. But it wasn't like I had many options. I felt the walls of the world closing in on me. So far I had wasted my young life with drugs, poor grades, and endless trouble for my parents. I was a disappointment. Maybe I was about to be punished for my sins against my father. Pops was driving and talking a mile a minute, giving me all kinds of advice about what to expect in the Army, but I barely heard a word. I just stared out of the passenger side window, silent, lost, and alone in my confused thoughts.

# ACT II

## You're in the Army Now

SEPTEMBER 7, 1987, WAS THE DAY THAT I REPORTED TO FORT SILL, Oklahoma, all pink-cheeked and ready for Boot Camp. As I exited the warm bus, a hot breeze welcomed me. Summers in Oklahoma, I learned, are blistering.

There is one small secret about the Army that recruiters fail to let you in on; it is that Army recruiters are lying bastards. Oh, it didn't dawn on me right away. My first two days of Basic Training were misleading. We got plenty of sleep, barely exercised, and to top it all off the drill sergeants treated us like kindly old uncles.

"Would you guys mind coming over here?" one of them nicely asked the platoon. It was refreshing to see that noncommissioned officers could also be gentlemen.

"I'm feeling this new Army," I whispered to my bunkmate, a nerdy white guy from North Dakota. I don't think there were any black men where he was from, because whenever I spoke, he looked at me as if I was a talking circus bear.

What initially impressed me about Basic Training was the food. I'd had nightmares that I would have to eat forty-year-old C-rations and dehydrated pork patties from WWI, but to my surprise we had steak and lobster.

Twenty-four hours later I was already waxing nostalgic about the good old days. Because on the third day of Basic Training, God created hell.

What I didn't know was that we weren't really in Basic Training, yet. We were only at the reception station, a sort of pre-boot camp registration. We filled out payroll and other forms, received our medical shots, and were issued camouflage fatigues, equipment, and the dreaded haircut also known as the "high and tight."

Once again, I want to stress that this was the '80s, so naturally I didn't have a natural when I was inducted. My hair was faded low on the sides, but on top was another discussion. I had let my hair grow long on top so that when I spritzed it heavily with World of Curls, I had a world of curls.

"Just a lil' off the top," I joked to the barber. After he was finished mutilating me, he held up a hand mirror so that I could admire his handiwork. What I saw in the mirror broke my heart.

"My head looks like a dick," I said, rubbing my hands over my gleaming pate. "You ain't getting a tip."

"Next!" the barber said dismissively.

Once we had finished with all of the paperwork, that's when the fun began. Our reception-station drill sergeants then marched us in a very undisciplined formation to an open field where a line of filthy, stinking cattle cars awaited. Filthy, stinking cattle cars are used to transport what? You guessed it—filthy, stinking cattle, so the sight of them made me a tad bit nervous. But what really scared the hell of out me were the Four Horsemen of the Apocalypse standing at attention in front of them.

"Meet your new drill sergeants," our old, kindly, uncle-like drill sergeant said.

"Huh?" Our formation let out a collective gasp. Standing before us were four of the biggest and blackest drill sergeants who ever drilled. Moments later, more drill sergeants stepped from out of the cattle cars. My knees wobbled as I bowed my head to pray.

What made them scarier was their silence. As we got on the cattle cars, they didn't say one word. Sweat streamed down my face and I was near tears. After traveling a few bumpy miles through the hot, dusty, and hilly Oklahoma countryside, I worked up the nerve to glance at the drill sergeant riding on our particular cattle car. He was tall, about 6'4", and it was obvious that his body was allergic to fat. He chewed Skoal and constantly spat out the cattle car's window. Streaks of his spittle sometimes splashed a recruit. None complained. This drill sergeant had an air of the desperado about him, and he wore the mirrored shades of a Southern sheriff, along with a Smokey the Bear drill sergeant's hat.

"Good afternoon, ladies," he growled, breaking the agonizing silence. "My name is Drill Sergeant Pipkin."

We stiffened, our mouths agape. Drill Sergeant Pipkin looked invincible, like he could eat lead and shit out number-two pencils.

"We've just crossed into Area 9000," he continued, bouncing up and down with the cattle car as it rumbled over some railroad tracks. His bearing was steely, his voice calm yet sounding rough as crunched gravel. "Your asses are now officially mine." He then fell silent, allowing ample time for our fragile minds to digest that important fact. We were, to a man, as terrified as a bunch of Sicilian brides on their wedding nights.

Seconds later the cattle car pulled to a stop, the doors somehow automatically opening. Drill Sergeant Pipkin spat out a perfect stream of Skoal juice and then casually adjusted his hat.

"Ladies, you have exactly ten seconds to exit my cattle car, and I have a secret for you—NINE OF THEM ARE GONE!!! GET OUT OF MY FUCKING CATTLE CAR YOU MAGGOTS!!! GET THE FUCK OUT OF MY CATTLE CAR!!!"

A split second later, fifty more drill sergeants materialized, yelling and yanking us out of the cattle cars. They ripped open our duffle bags and threw the contents in the air. Some recruits tripped and fell. Hats were being knocked off heads. It was pandemonium. None of the recruits knew where or how to stand.

"Don't you eyeball me, maggot," I overheard a drill sergeant yell at one recruit.

Another recruit made the mistake of bending over to catch his breath. A short muscular drill was all over him in a split second, snatching him up by his collar. "Stand up straight, gonorrhea boy. What are you, the hunchback of Notre friggin' Dame?" The drill sergeants seemed to say friggin' a lot.

Next to me stood a behemoth chewing out a private for packing unauthorized items. His drawl was pure Old South. One by one he launched the items across the parking lot like grenades. "Cologne? Pajamas? Friggin' house slippers? Who in the hell do you think you are, peter puffer, Hugh friggin' Hefner?"

The drill sergeant pointed at the ground, the universal signal to "beat your face," or do pushups. The recruit started crying. I smiled at his misfortune—but then King Kong's younger brother got all up in my face. I glanced at his name patch—Drill Sergeant Billups. I filed away the name of the man who was about to murder me.

"Something funny, ass-breath?" he asked.

I gulped and shook my head no. Drill Sergeant Billups inched closer to me, his gaze reptilian, his hot spicy breath slowly invading my nostrils. I winced.

"Then what's your problem, shit for brains?"

I attempted to speak but he cut me off.

"Were you 'bout to call me an asshole?" he snapped, big thick veins bulging in his big thick neck. "Shitbird."

I violently shook my head.

"I think you were about to call me an asshole." He was so convincing that for a split second I thought, *maybe I was about to call him an asshole.*

He smacked me upside the head and right out my daydream. "Hey dick-face, I see that you have a rectal cranial inversion, but you better your get your head out of your ass and in the game."

I nodded as I casually adjusted my glasses.

"What in the hell is on your fat face, private?" Drill Sergeant Billups barked.

I was silent, not knowing what he was referring to.

He snatched off my designer prescription glasses. "These! This is not Army issue, broke-dick."

Drill Sergeant Billups turned and held up the glasses and said loudly, "This fat-ass gummy bear thinks he's special."

The other drills egged him on. "Yeah, he's an in-di-vidual."

I stood there panicking because I couldn't see a damn thing. All I could hear was the cacophony of yells. I was near-sighted and had always worn glasses, but I was now learning that civilian glasses weren't allowed while in Basic Training. The Army would issue me its own pair of monstrous-looking spectacles. I would learn that these were called birth-control glasses, because no self-respecting woman would copulate with a guy who wore them. Drill Sergeant Billups threw my $200 Ralph Laurens on the ground and crushed them underneath his jump boots.

Pissed, I mumbled, "*My momma bought me those glasses.*"

"'My momma bought me those glasses,'" he mocked. "Your momma is about to buy you an army-issued ass-whipping. Get on your fat face, limp-dick," Drill Sergeant Billups ordered.

*There is no way I will make it through eight weeks of this*, I thought as I pushed my way to China. And this was just Basic Training '80s style. I had heard horror stories about drill sergeants beating recruits half to death in the '70s and '60s.

The rest of the day was a blur of arranging our gear in the barracks, marching lessons, and overall screwing up of every order the drill sergeants gave us. By the time 10:00 pm ("lights out" in Army lingo) rolled around, I was battered, bruised, and beat down. Lying on my bunk in the darkness, I suppressed the urge to cry. As I pulled the green army-issue wool blanket over my tired body, I felt like a total failure.

IN THE ARMY, I HAD TO LEARN A WHOLE NEW LANGUAGE. The bathroom became a "latrine" or "head." My bed was a "rack." A hat was "headgear"; a uniform was a "BDU," short for battle dress uniform. What about the virtuous young lady waiting on me back at home? According to the drill sergeants, her new name was good ole' "Mary Jane Rotten Crotch."

However, the most important thing I learned on my first full day in the Army was that I did not want to be in the Army. Standing ankle-deep in a muddy field doing deep knee bends and pushups in a driving rainstorm has a way of coloring your outlook.

"I bet you dumbasses wish you'd paid more attention in high school, huh?" Drill Sergeant Billups lectured us that first morning. "I can't hear you maggots counting.

"You're fucked now," he continued. "See what a low GPA gets you? You're not in Kansas anymore, Dorothy. You and Toto are now in a world of shit."

Drill Sergeant Billups, clad in a waterproof poncho, casually walked between the rows of pushupping recruits, his boots splashing clumps of mud in our faces.

"Just look at you maggots. What a disgusting stack of rat shit y'all turned out to be. I bet your single-parent-ass mommas wished abortions were legal the year she shitted y'all out."

"Yes, Drill Sergeant," we gasped.

It was at that point that I wished my father was friends with a congressman. As I struggled doing my pushups, I knew there was no way these drills could hate me as much as they seemed to. How could they? We'd never met before.

"Harmon?" Billups glowered over me.

"Yes, sir?" I screamed, my voice straining from the hoarseness.

He exploded. "Sir? Don't call me 'sir,' fat ass. I'm not an officer. I work for a living. You address me as 'drill sergeant,' and if your illiterate ass can't say that, then just call me God. You got that, stool breath?"

My weak arms strained to hold up me up. "Yes, sir... no, I... uh, I mean yes, Sergeant God."

"Harmon, you're fat and pathetic. Your new name is Re-run," Drill Sergeant Billups ordered. "Is that okay with you?"

"Yes, Drill Sergeant." But it really wasn't okay with me. I wanted a cool nickname like Killer or Rambo, not the name of the fat dude from *What's Happening?*

Drill Sergeant Billups just sneered and walked over to the next lucky contestant.

"And what's your name, asswipe?"

"Private Henson Drill Sergeant!" the young, skinny, pimply-faced white recruit screamed.

"'Private Henson Drill Sergeant?'" Billups mocked in an exaggerated, high-pitched voice. "Boy, you sound like a queer. You ever play football?"

"Yes, Drill Sergeant," Private Henson answered.

Billups smirked. "I bet you were a tight end, huh? "

"No, not with that ass," Drill Sergeant Smith chimed in. "He looks like a wide receiver."

"From now on your name is Head Quick, cuz I bet you are quick to give a guy head."

Drill Sergeant Billups continued down the line giving out racist and homophobic nicknames like Juan Valdez, Hitler, Samurai Sam, Hawaii Five-O, and Greg Up-Your-Anus. He also informed us that for the next eight weeks there would be no spending of money other than on basic toiletries, and no sweets, alcohol, music, magazines, or entertainment of any kind, other than for the enjoyment of the drill sergeants. We would also be told when to get up, when to go to sleep, when to eat, when to wash, and when to use the latrine. The only thing separating us from jail was the absence of bars.

By the second week, my ears and ass had been turned into ground beef thanks to the constant chewing of the drill sergeants. The yelling began at 4 am, usually preceded by the loud banging of a nightstick being smashed against an aluminum trashcan.

"All right ladies, drop your cocks and put on your socks!" they'd yell.

The rest of the day was a cloud of yelling, chow, more yelling, training, chow, even more yelling, weapons cleaning, chow, and if you could believe it, more yelling, boot shining, then finally passing out at 10 pm, only to repeat the cycle again the next day. Some nights, when the drills were feeling especially sinister, they'd wait until we'd fall asleep , then burst back into our rooms and drag us back out to the parking lot to do calisthenics for the next hour. I was in a constant state of exhaustion. I felt like a prisoner of war.

One of the bright spots about Basic Training was getting to know the other recruits. I met some interesting guys from all over. There was Private Grass, a white dude from Maine. He was the only recruit to get a letter every day, always from his girlfriend. Grass lorded that fact over us, too, even going so far as reading her letters out loud. We were jealous. One day's mail call brought her photo. We passed it around the platoon like a joint.

"Grassy ass, is that your girlfriend?" Drill Sergeant Pipkin said, snatching the photo from a recruit.

Grass smiled proudly, taking the bait. "Yes, Drill Sergeant."

Pipkin leaned in and squinted at the picture. "BeJaysus... that's one ugly bitch."

Grass never shared another letter.

Private Mancebo was a Dominican from Boston who did the best Tony Montana impersonation I'd ever seen. He'd walk around the showers holding his penis and delivering lines like, "Say hello to my lil' friend."

My roommate's name was Private Green. This guy was special and had a good heart. I knew it right away when he showed me his prom pictures.

"This is my girl, Phyllis," he said proudly, chest puffed out. Phyllis was a brown-skinned cutie. She looked marvelous in her black strapless prom dress. But I was at loss for words while I studied the picture. Clearly, Phyllis only had one arm.

"She's, uh, beautiful," I finally said. But drill sergeants, just like kids, can be so cruel. One day during room inspection, Drill Sergeant Billups noticed Phyllis's picture taped to the inside of Green's wall locker.

"Damn, son, your girl is 'armed' and dangerous," he cracked. "Your new name is Captain Hook."

We had plenty of characters. Like the Spunkmaster, a pockmarked kid from Minnesota or someplace like that. He got caught whacking off in a latrine stall. A recruit from Hawaii snuck into the stall next to him, stood on the toilet, and snapped his picture with a Polaroid.

"Say cheese," he joked before running outside and waving the picture to dry it. The entire platoon gathered around him and watched the picture develop. As the image slowly dissolved into focus, we cracked up. There on the toilet and looking up into the camera sat a very surprised and very orgasmic Spunkmaster, his spunk all over the stall. No one else ever used that stall again.

Then there was Private Henson. Ever since Drill Sergeant Billups had made him the butt of a gay joke, Henson had gone off the deep end. He actively tried to get himself "chaptered," or kicked out of the Army. Henson was a world-class screw-up. A real shitbird. The guy broke every rule in the book, always getting us into trouble for some infraction. I say "us" because if one recruit messed up, the rest of us—and not the offending recruit—had to pay the price.

"Thank you, Private Henson," we'd politely say while doing grass drills and pushups under a blazing sun because of one of his many mistakes. This as Private Henson sat in the shade relaxing, sipping cool water from his canteen. Drill sergeants did this so that recruits would eventually police each other. We did. One night our resident headcase got a headache, along with a blanket party. While he slept, a group of recruits beat the hell out of him with soap bars wrapped in pillowcases.

The next day, Private Henson attempted suicide, the operative word being "attempted." He was upstairs busily buffing the third-floor hallway when he decided to twist part of the long buffer cord into a makeshift noose and then slip it around his scrawny neck. Private Henson then wedged the buffer underneath a bed and jumped out of a nearby window. Most of the platoon was outside spit-shining our boots when he took flight.

"Aaaaaaaaaaahh!" he yelled.

There was one slight problem. Private Henson jumped from the third floor, but he had about five floors worth of cord attached to his neck.

He hit the pavement; legs splaying at impossible angles while excess cord slowly coiled around him.

Someone ran for help and came back with Drill Sergeant Pipkin. The tall drill instructor stood over Private Henson and shook his head disgustedly.

"What a fuckup," he sighed. "Can't even kill himself right."

Another early highlight of Basic Training was the Patriotism Class. After more than 200 years of practice, the United States Army has perfected the art of psychological warfare, most of it aimed at its own soldiers. The Patriotism Class was one of the few courses that didn't take place in the mud. We were excited when the drill sergeants marched us into the base theater. But any thought of a leisurely afternoon watching a flick were dashed when in a scene lifted right out the movie *Patton*, our commanding officer strode onstage with the American flag waving on the screen in the background. Stoic and grizzled, our colonel looked as if he could be fresh from a faraway battlefield.

"We are doing God's dirty work," he told us. I squirmed as he made the case that a soldier's cause was noble and honorable. He was adamant that America had the divine and moral authority to police the world. To die in defense of our nation's ideals was the only way for a real soldier to die. There were plenty of raised eyebrows amongst the recruits.

"They are trying to brainwash us," I whispered to Green. But he was starstruck and paid me no attention. I too marveled at the officer's performance. The military is stocked with plenty of soldiers like him. They are usually tall, fit individuals with a bearing that screams leadership. As a young man, it was hard not to be impressed with the older men who have made it their lives' work to lead young men into combat. They have a potent combination of ego and personal conviction. I have to admit, after a while I was also hanging on the colonel's every word. He controlled us with the skill of a country evangelist. After he finished speaking, we were shown a slickly produced documentary. It contained scenes made up from every major military campaign the army had ever taken part in. On the screen flashed moving images of men heroically dying in battles from the Revolutionary War all the way up to Vietnam. They did a real job on us that afternoon. We went right from the theater to bayonet training. Like the other recruits, I slashed the stuffing out of the practice dummies. Later that night, I dreamed of hand-to-hand combat with the Russians.

A MONTH LATER, I WAS WONDERING WHY I STILL HADN'T BEEN promoted to general. The perpetual soldier's scowl I wore on my face made it obvious to all that I was born to kill.

"We're here to make war, not love," I barked at the platoon.

"Ooh...Rah!" they answered as one.

As a newly minted assistant platoon guide, I was tasked to oversee the troops when the drill sergeants were not around. It was an honor, and I thought I had earned it.

"Harmon?" Drill Sergeant Pipkin roared one morning, pulling me out of formation. He stood me at attention in front of the platoon. "You're the least fucked up of all of these here fuckups. Plus you're the biggest. So, I'm putting you in charge."

That meant I would now march the platoon to and from chow. I would also make sure their uniforms were "squared away" or adhered to regulations, and report any problems to the drill sergeants. I sometimes led the recruits in singing cadence. It was a coveted position, one handed down to only the most motivated of recruits. In four short weeks, I had mastered many intricate techniques of warfare. Sun Tzu and Clausewitz would have been proud. I was the perfect soldier, except for one thing—I couldn't shoot the side of a barn if I was standing right in front of it.

My shortcoming was revealed during BRM, also known as Basic Rifle Marksmanship. BRM was one of the most important weeks of Basic Training. It was when a recruit finally learned how to kill or at least maim the enemy. We learned the fundamentals of bayonet fighting and how to break down and qualify firing the M16A2 rifle. The pressure was tremendous. To qualify, a recruit had to hit at least twenty-three targets out of forty. Sounds easy. Trust me, it's not—especially when you have a drill sergeant whispering in your ear that you are one of the worst recruits ever to squeeze a trigger.

If a recruit failed to qualify, he was "recycled" to a platoon that was four weeks behind his current one. Basically, the recruit had to start Basic Training all over again. To be recycled was a fate worse than death. By the week of BRM, a recruit had pretty much adjusted to Army life, and had also forged some really close bonds with his fellow recruits. To be forced to start over with a new and less-seasoned platoon was crushing.

There was no way that I'd be able cope with being recycled. For one, I was a leader in the platoon. Most of the drill sergeants only disliked me, as opposed to the outright hatred they displayed to the rest of the platoon. I helped to set the standards for the other recruits. They looked up to me. I would have rather quit than start over, and I knew I couldn't go back home if I quit.

My mantra of "undesired results" didn't apply to failing BRM. That would be a true failure.

Our training to fire the M16A2 rifle was meticulous. We learned how to break the weapon down to its bare components and put it back together, blindfolded. This weapon can fire ninety rounds a minute and has a maximum range of nearly 2,000 feet. Before we even had a chance to load a round in the weapon's magazine, we had to learn how to breathe while firing it, as well as the proper stance and body positioning. And we rehearsed, over and over again.

The day we finally got our first chance to qualify, I was so confident that I felt like I could shoot the eye out of a fly at hundred yards at night while blindfolded and drunk. As a platoon guide, I was in the first firing group.

"I'm the black Sergeant York," I bragged as I slammed the magazine of forty rounds into my weapon, alluding to the legendary World War I marksman.

"Yeah? Let's see what you got, Ram-bro," Drill Sergeant Billups said sarcastically.

I scanned down range while the operator in the tower began the countdown. It was at least 95 degrees, and beads of sweat dampened my forehead.

"Ready on the firing line?" the voiced squawked through the loudspeakers. "Five, Four, Three."

I blocked out all thoughts and steadied my breathing, remembering my training. With the earplugs screwed in tight, my heartbeat vibrated like a conga drum in my chest.

"Two, One."

My finger gently caressed the trigger while my eye was firmly trained on my weapon's sight. I knew the pop-up silhouette targets would be laid out at distances of 50, 75, 150, 200, and 300 meters. Also, at some point multiple targets would pop up at the same time, forcing me to make split-second decisions. I settled myself in the foxhole, feet planted firmly. I looked at my watch. It was 9:12 am. I checked the wind. There was none. I let out a deep sigh and tried to visualize hitting the targets. I was ready.

"Fire!"

The crackle of gunfire was deafening and rounds pinged sharply off the metal targets ricocheting in the dirt.

The first target was a gimme.

Take that, I thought, imagining the targets were drill sergeants.

The next target was at 300 meters. I missed, badly.

That's okay, B., I thought. You'll get the next one.

A target at 200 meters popped up. Again I missed, then again and again and again.

"What the —?" I said under my breath, but kept firing. The targets were popping up with greater frequency. I began to squint, and then I lost my composure and started hitting other recruits' targets.

"Focus!" Drill Sergeant Billups ordered, slapping the back of my Kevlar helmet.

"Cease fire! Cease fire!" came the word from the tower.

When the smoke cleared, I had only hit thirteen targets.

"Sergeant York, my black ass," Drill Sergeant Billups snickered. "Get out of my foxhole."

I was in shock. What had I done wrong? I went over everything in my mind and I couldn't figure out why I shot so poorly.

All was not lost, though, because we had two chances to qualify. But I would have to wait until the afternoon. That gave me a few hours to practice and to be taunted by the drill sergeants.

"Harmon?" It was Drill Sergeant Smith. He *did* hate my guts, for real.

I snapped to attention. "Yes, Drill Sergeant."

"Delta Platoon has a spot waiting for you," he laughed before walking off barking like a dog.

I lowered my head in shame. Delta Platoon was the recycle platoon, the dreaded Delta dogs. I promised myself that I would not screw up a second time.

As I steadied myself in foxhole #12 that afternoon, I mentally plastered Drill Sergeant Smith's face on every target.

"Fire!"

I hit the first four targets and that boosted my confidence. But with every high came a devastating low.

"Damn," I muttered, missing yet another target. I had lost count of how many I'd hit. Time was running out.

Moments later came the order. "Cease fire! Cease fire!"

I held my breath for my final count.

"Number twelve," the loudspeaker crackled.

I swallowed hard.

"Twenty targets," the tower operator said.

My face fell to my hands. I was crushed and wanted to crawl deeper into the foxhole.

"Get out, get your sorry ass out of my friggin' foxhole!" Drill Sergeant Billups snapped, before snatching off my red platoon guide armband. "You don't deserve this."

I tried to hold my head high but I couldn't look anyone in the eye. The guys I walked past patted me on back.

"Tough break, B.," some sympathized.

"It's gon' be all right," others lied.

I wasn't allowed to ride back in the first truck with those who qualified. I had to ride back to the barracks with the half-dozen other recruits who also didn't qualify. No one spoke of being recycled, but it was on all of our minds. I was ashamed. I'd failed under pressure. If this had been a real battle, I would have let my comrades down. As I looked around the truck at the sad pathetic recruits, some of them well-known, true-blue fuckups, I thought of how far and how fast my star had just fallen.

**F**OR THE REST OF THE DAY, I FELT LIKE I WAS TREATED LIKE THE CRAZY aunt who lived in the room upstairs. The other recruits avoided me for fear of contamination. In reality, most of them just didn't know what to say to me, and vice versa. I was devastated. I retreated into myself and stoically endured the isolation. The closest I came to being in the group was marching with them back to barracks. Talk about a demotion. Earlier that morning I was marching them.

As the evening wore on, I kept waiting for the other boot to drop. None of the drill sergeants told me when I would be transferred to Delta Platoon. But I knew it was coming. My roommates were outside congregating with the other recruits, cracking jokes and roughhousing. I didn't blame them—a morgue-like stench hung in the air of our room. Meanwhile, I sat on my bunk, stomach twisted into a knot, and waited. I flinched each time the squad door opened.

Then the door squeaked open and I held my breath. It was Drill Sergeant Pipkin. He'd become the drill sergeant that I was the coolest with over the course of Basic.

"How do you feel?" Drill Sergeant Pipkin asked. I was taken aback by his tone. It was almost, well, almost normal.

"Terrible, Drill Sergeant," I answered.

He put his boot on the footboard of my bunk, and balanced himself by leaning forward, his arm on his knee. "You should feel terrible. You royally fucked up, son. You let us all down. The other drill sergeants and I had a lot of faith in you. We thought you were pretty squared away."

I just nodded, unsure of what to say. It took everything in my power not to cry.

"You're getting one more chance," he said.

My eyes lit up. "Another chance, Drill Sergeant?"

"Did I fuckin' stutter, Private?"

"No, Drill Sergeant."

"Next Saturday, you and the other fuckups are going to march down to the range and get one more shot. If you fail this time, you better learn how to bark."

And with that he walked out, slamming the door behind him for effect.

Seeing the drill sergeant leave, the guys who were standing outside raced into the room. It was Green, Hill, Sierra, who was the platoon guide, and Mancebo, the recruits I was closest to.

"What did he say?" Green asked.

I exhaled a huge sigh, still not believing my good fortune. "I'm getting one more chance to qualify."

They all gave me pounds and hugs. "You'll do it. We'll make sure."

"Lights out, ladies!" Drill Sergeant Smith ordered later that night, clicking off the switch. "Hey, Harmon?"

"Yes, Drill Sergeant," I answered, my voice echoing in the darkness.

"I hope you like Alpo," he joked. "Because after you fuck up again next week, that's what you're gong to be eating. Woof! Woof!"

I bolted upright out of sleep and shook the nightmare's images of barking dogs out of my mind and wiped the sweat from my forehead. I sighed and looked at my snoring roommates. This was becoming a nightly routine. It's hard to sleep when you know the exact date you're going to die.

That's how I felt knowing that in a few days, life as I knew it would be changed forever. I had resolved that if I didn't qualify, I was going to either kill myself or get myself kicked out. I was dead serious. It would be death before dishonor.

In my entire life, I never felt as much pressure as I did that week. I was terrified and had a constant lump in my throat. My grip on sanity was slowly unhinging. Qualifying was on my mind nearly every waking moment, especially when I would see the fresh faces of the Delta Platoon marching by.

"See them, Harmon?" Drill Sergeant Smith cruelly pointed. "That's gon' be you." He then barked again for emphasis.

The other drill sergeants were just as bad. They screwed with me every chance they got, a bark here, a howl there. The CIA would have been proud of their psychological tricks. I couldn't understand they were treating me so cruelly. It was like they were rooting for me to fail.

It turned out that Pops was a big help. Each night I'd shuffle to the pay phones with a pocketful of quarters and make a call to home. My father's pep talks kept me going. He was my lifeline.

"I got faith in you, son," he'd tell me. Pops had faith in me? He had never said that before. I had to qualify. I couldn't let him down again.

It was also the first time that I really and truly felt the awesome power of God. I mean that real, authentic, shivers-down-your-spine power. I prayed so much that week. I fasted, and I even carried a small Bible in my uniform's left chest pocket at all times. Other recruits frequently saw me in a trancelike state silently reading through the pages of the Book of Psalms.

I made sure that I was prepared for my blind date with destiny. I trained meticulously all week and absorbed every scrap of information about my rifle. The day of our qualification was a beautiful one. It was sunny and the temperature hovered near 75 degrees. It was, as Crazy Horse supposedly used to say, a good day to die.

The drill sergeants made us march to the range—eight miles away.

"Y'all don't deserve to ride in my truck," Drill Sergeant Billups said.

Once there, we wasted no time. There were seven of us and we quickly settled into the foxholes. I was in foxhole #5. The drill sergeants watched us closely as we sighted our rifles. Drill Sergeant Pipkin noticed something fishy about my weapon.

"Gimme that weapon," he said, snatching it from my outstretched hands.

He looked it over and aimed it.

"Harmon? Was your weapon sighted like this last week?"

"Yes, Drill Sergeant."

He had a look of pure incredulousness on his face. "Jesus, son, you got your weapon sighted ass-backwards."

The M16A2 rifle has two adjustable sights—front and rear. Elevation adjustments are made using the front sight, and elevation changes and windage adjustments are made using the rear sight. It is imperative that you sight your weapon properly; if it's not, you will rarely hit what you're aiming for.

"Ahh," I said. The magnitude of what I had done hit me like a lightning bolt. I felt beyond stupid for screwing up such a crucial step. That glitch was the cause of my present situation. Drill Sergeant Pipkin adjusted my sights properly and handed the rifle back to me. The tower counted us down. "Ready on the firing line."

*God,* I silently prayed, *I need your help.*

"Fire!"

I squeezed the trigger as if my life depended on it. I was a machine. I was knocking down so many targets that I lost count. I was so in the zone I even let a couple of 300m targets alone to concentrate on the closer, easier ones. It was as if I could see the bullets streaking toward the targets.

"Cease fire! Cease fire!"

My hands shook as I took out my earplugs and gasped for breath. My heart rate was off the charts. Slowly the official in the tower revealed the results. Three of the first four recruits had made it, with one failing.

"Okay, God," I whispered. It had finally come down to this, a week of practice, prayer, and pressure.

"Foxhole #5," the tower crackled. His voice was in slow motion and I hung on every word. I held my breath. "Thirty-eight targets."

"Thirty-eight?" I jumped in the air. "Yes!"

Drill Sergeant Pipkin was just as surprised.

"Well, hot damn, Harmon," he said, slapping me on the back. "You have successfully unfucked yourself."

I was so happy, I nearly cried. When the pressure was on, I didn't fold. In all honesty, I nearly had a nervous breakdown there at the age of seventeen. The whole week became a seminal moment in my life, a frame of reference that I would use to compare when dealing with future turbulent times. I thanked God for giving me strength. Without sounding overly dramatic, it was my first true experience of how God could affect my life. I never would have made it without the power of prayer.

My friends were waiting when I got back.

"Well?" Private Sierra asked.

"I made it!" I grinned, while they enveloped me with hugs and pounds. "I made it!"

Later that night, Drill Sergeant Smith walked into my room. He looked me up and down as I stood at attention. He casually threw the red assistant platoon guide armband on my bunk then walked out without saying a word.

THE REST OF BASIC TRAINING WAS, WELL, PRETTY BASIC. I marched through the last few weeks with ease, and this time I didn't have to lie to graduate. I was even one of two recruits who were promoted to E-2, the second rank that a private can attain. My family drove up to Oklahoma for the ceremony. My mother bawled like a little girl. Andre and Marshall were noticeably proud of their newly lean and fit brother.

"Son, I am so proud of you," Pops gushed, his eyes moist.

I hugged him tight. "I couldn't have done it without you, Pops. I love you so much."

He looked me in the eye and smiled. "I love you too, son."

We had changed. Over the countless phone calls during boot camp, we seemed to forget the past and became close again. I felt like that little kid again, the one who used to go fishing with his father. It was the beginning of another new relationship with Pops.

Basic Training was also the catalyst for a profound change in my personality. My "quit" trait was gone. What I originally perceived as hatred directed at me from Drill Sergeants Pipkin, Billups, Smith, and the others was actually a caring desire to see us succeed not only in the Army but also in life. After the graduation ceremony, I nearly fainted when they began speaking to and treating us as human beings. We were soldiers now and were to be accorded the proper respect, they told us. I was proud to know them. They had pushed me to the limits of my mental and physical abilities. I became more organized, more goal-oriented. For the first time in my life, I had real discipline.

The next phase was called Advanced Individual Training, or AIT. That's where, for the next six weeks, we learned our job specialty.

Someone once said that the Army was the incompetent leading the unwilling to do the unnecessary in an unbelievable amount of time. After the first day of AIT, I concurred. I was to become a "forward observer," a high-tech name for crash-test dummy.

Basically, during an operation [suicide], I was forward of the front lines observing [spying on] the enemy. This put me in the nexus [anus] of the action…lucky me. All I was armed with were an M16 [useless], a pair of binoculars [cool], and some clunky high-powered laser guiding equipment [never worked].

"What, no slingshot?" I sarcastically asked the instructor.

Once I located a target, my mission was to radio in its location and adjust fire from 155mm howitzers, A-10 jets, Apache helicopters, or battleships out at sea. It was exciting to see the massive explosions during training, but we were shocked into reality when our instructor revealed to us that the life expectancy of a forward observer during combat was nine seconds. He laughed, knowing that we were silently cursing our recruiters.

"From here on, there will be no more lies," he joked.

But there was no need for the devil to lie to you anymore once you were in hell.

Christmas gave us our first break from the rigors of training. After eleven weeks of torture, I looked forward to a few weeks of R&R as a civilian. Once back in the safe confines of Guinn Street, I savored all the flavors and sounds of the neighborhood. The people were the same but the flowers seemed more vibrant, the leaves greener, and the air crisper. My mother was even nicer.

"What do you want me to cook for breakfast, son?" she asked.

I almost suffered whiplash from the double-take. I couldn't ever remember my mother asking for my input on a meal. My little brother Marshall ran to the store for me. I was the man of the hour. I had to go and serve my country in order to get served by my family. Pops hadn't even banged on my bedroom door at 6 am.

All of my friends were home from college. Nelson had scholarship offers from all of the top football programs in the nation, but had chosen to stay close to home and attend Grambling University. His brother Craig tagged along with him. My buddy Dale went to McNeese State, a local college in town. Harold and LaRon both had jobs in Lake Charles.

I tried to pick up where we left off, but it just wasn't the same. Although it had only been a few months, we had outgrown each other. A lot of my friends still wanted to get high, but I had rehabbed courtesy of Uncle Sam. After Basic Training, I couldn't bear the thought of doing drugs, and besides, I had too much on the line. If I came up hot on a urinalysis, I would be dishonorably discharged. The guys tried to egg me on, but my willpower was too strong.

I soon got the feeling I was getting on their nerves with my new attitude. I teased them when they wolfed down Big Macs, chastised them when they guzzled cheap beer and wine. They reminded me that their vices used to be my vices. But that was the old Byron. I was now lean and had the healthy, raw-boned look of a seventeen-year-old soldier.

I spoke of goals and missions. They spoke of girls and sexual positions. I had seen things they would never see, done things they would never do. They still chipped in together on buying a forty-ounce bottle of Old English 800 malt liquor, for God's sake. I could now afford to buy my own.

That was the beginning of what I would call the Big Disconnect. From henceforth, things would never be the same for the boys from Guinn Street.

The highlight of my holiday break was a party that my brother Andre and his friend Roman threw for me at our house. Pops spent the night at a hotel while we basically kept my mother duct-taped to a chair in the back bedroom. There were hundreds of people from all over Louisiana and as far away as Texas. The front and back yards were filled with whole fraternities and sororities stepping. Girls I had dreamed about while in high school were flirting with the new me. I loved all of the attention. Alas, the next day I had to ship out. This time, it would be for a few years overseas. My mother and I reenacted our earlier goodbye when I went to boot camp, tear for tear.

After AIT, I was assigned to the 3rd Infantry Division and shipped overseas to Schweinfurt, Germany, a bustling little town a hundred miles east of Frankfurt. Located right in the gut of the country, Schweinfurt's ball-bearing plants made it a prime target for bombing by the English during World War II. My home for the next two years would be Ledward Barracks, home of my new unit, 1/10th FA (the first battalion of the tenth field artillery), aka "The Dime."

By joining the Army, I knew there was a chance that I'd see combat. I just didn't know that I'd see it on my own base. Ledward Barracks was a small post, only a few thousand soldiers, but it was like Dodge City. I can remember the prophetic words of the personnel sergeant who processed my orders when I landed at Rhein Mein airport in Frankfurt.

"Ledward Barracks?" he said, quickly stamping the sheets of paper and then pointing me toward the bus. "Good luck and keep your head down."

As the bus carrying the new guys drove through the Ledward Barracks' gates, we noticed a group of chiseled soldiers clad in orange shorts with shaved heads picking up trash and double-timing all over post. They must have been insane. It was snowing.

"Who are they...Rangers?" asked a soldier sitting behind the bus driver.

The driver smiled. "No. Prisoners." There was so much crime being committed by soldiers on and off post that Ledward had its own prison.

The base was home to a handful of legendary artillery, infantry, and cavalry units. All had made their bones during every war since World War I. All had sordid reputations on base too, but one of the worst was the The Dime. Our unit's unofficial motto was, "First off The Dime, first in crime."

As we exited the bus in front of Headquarters barracks, duffle bags slung over our shoulders, we newbies were met with less than friendly stares.

"Fresh meat," one soldier yelled from a second floor window.

One fat, scruffy corporal looked at me and licked his lips.

*I'm never taking a shower here*, I thought, wishing I had a shank.

Just my luck. It was like K-MART, the sequel. While I settled in, Private First Class Buffalino, aka Buff, my new roommate, gave me a short history lesson. Over the last few years, soldiers from The Dime were rumored to have committed a number of murders, rapes, arsons, knifings, and robberies. A couple of weeks prior to my arrival, two former soldiers from The Dime had been extradited from Fort Lewis, an Army base near Seattle. They had raped and dismembered a handicapped girl, then wrapped her body in an Army poncho liner and threw it in the Rhine River.

"I can't wait to get outta here," Buff admitted.

"When do you leave?" I asked, unpacking my duffle bags.

He held up three fingers.

"Three years?"

He shook his head. "Three months."

Lucky bastard—I was facing three years. I felt like a new inmate who was assigned to a cell with a guy who was getting out the next morning.

The Dime was split into five sections, and all felt their two cents were worth more. There were the four artillery or "gun" batteries: Alpha, Bravo, Charlie, and Delta. The last section was the Headquarters battery, aka Hollywood, where I was assigned. There was an intense rivalry between Headquarters and the gun batteries. Our Army MOS designation was 13 Foxtrot and theirs was 13 Bravo. The 13 Bravos thought 13 Foxtrots were soft because our jobs relied so much on technology, and theirs was all about raw power. They loaded heavy rounds into howitzers while we rode around in comfortable Hummers equipped with laser-guided systems.

"They build the pyramids, but we are the architects," was how one sergeant explained it to me.

The13 Bravos were also upset because most of them didn't score high enough on their ASVAB entry exams to qualify for our MOS. We called them DAGBs—short for Dumb-Ass Gun Bunnies.

I was assigned to my section's A team, which consisted of myself; Buff, who was a short, white private first class from upstate New York; Specialist 4 Anderson, an Eddie Murphy look-alike from Long Island who was one of the worst military men since Gomer Pyle and appeared to live in sick call; and Corporal King, a black, burnt-out former sergeant from Brooklyn who had gotten busted for some infraction. King rejoiced when he first met me.

"Finally, I got me a new bitch to do all my work," he grinned, slapping me on the back. And work I did, at least until I got me a new bitch to do all of my work. Those were the rules.

I really didn't care. I had grown to love the Army. I wanted to be the world's best soldier. My uniform was always starched, my boots were perpetually shined to a gloss, and I studied my manuals every chance I could. I knew my job duties backwards and forwards and after only a few months was promoted to private first class. At this pace I'd make sergeant in three years, the earliest possible time for a soldier in my job specialty. I wanted to renegotiate my enlistment contract and re-up for twenty years.

My supervisor was a black super-trooper aptly named Sergeant Paul Wayne. He was from Pennsylvania and, at twenty-four years old, one of the youngest sergeants in the unit. All spit-shine and polish, he lived, ate, and breathed the Army. However, he had an uncanny ability to make anyone of a lower rank instantly hate him, myself included.

"You better watch him," King warned. "He thinks we're at West Point."

Wayne treated us as if we were still in Basic Training, going so far as having surprise inspections on weekend mornings. Although I myself was something of a super-trooper in training, Sergeant Wayne eventually made me hate everything about the Army.

I MANAGED TO GET THROUGH MY FIRST MONTH ON LEDWARD WITHOUT getting shanked. In no time at all I had settled in and made a number of friends, although in The Dime there was really only one type of crowd to hang out with—the wrong one. My new buddies wasted no time in introducing me to the wondrous delights of the local red-light district.

"Where we going?" I asked one Friday. My buddies looked at each other and laughed.

Private First Class Frank, a smooth brother from Houston, winked and said, "Frankfurt."

The guys became excited. They were backslapping and high-fiving each other. "What's so special about Frankfurt?" I asked.

"Ho' houses," Private First Class Moore explained, playfully punching my right arm. Moore was a high-strung budding rapper from Detroit—or, as he called it, "De-twah."

I sucked my teeth. "Whorehouses? I ain't paying for any broads."

They laughed again, with Frank laughing the loudest. "That's what we said when we first got here, too," he said knowingly.

By the time we had walked through two blocks of the red-light district, I was wishing I had brought more cash. The bright lights and neon signs advertising sex were overwhelming. There were discos, bars, brothels, and sex shops everywhere. We tried to pace ourselves, briefly walking in and out of a few different places. Buzzing from tequila shots, I marveled at the array of beautiful half-naked women of all nationalities standing seductively outside the rooms, their assets on full display.

"I want to marry you," I lip-synched to a curvy Latin beauty sitting on a chair with her legs wide open. She blew me a kiss. I caught it and blew one back.

"I'm in love with a whore," I drunkenly confessed to Frank.

"But you haven't seen anything yet," he replied.

I rolled my eyes. "It can't possibly get any better than her."

Frank was silent…until we were in the lobby of the world-famous Eros Center.

"Are you ready?" he asked. He acted is if we were in a football huddle during a big game.

I nodded.

"He ain't ready," Moore joked.

By the time we made it to the first floor, I realized that I wasn't ready.

The inside of the Eros Center was bathed in red light and laid out like a large motel, with the scantily clad ladies of the evening standing outside the doors of the tiny rooms. While loud disco music pulsed in the background, we browsed among the merchandise. Here and there I snuck a peek inside the rooms. The accommodations were spartan, just big enough room for a tiny bed, a sink, and a dresser. The first floor was filled with all European white women. There were a few late models, but mainly all I saw were Model T's. Most of them looked like Eastern European shot-put champions.

I frowned. "Pass."

The selection improved dramatically on the second floor—that's where all the Hispanic women were. Meringue music was blasting from the sound system. The floor had a Carnival atmosphere to it.

"Hey, Papi," a slender raven-haired vixen whispered.

"*Bonjour*," Moore answered.

Frank and I did a double-take at Moore's *faux pas*.

"Sorry," Moore corrected himself. "I meant *arrivederci*."

All of the ladies looked like worthy charities, and I was itching to make a donation.

"Not yet," Frank advised.

By now I was good and sloshed. I became indignant and looked at him cross-eyed. "If not now, dammit, then when? And if not her, goddammit, then who?"

He and Moore laughed and dragged me up the stairs. I blinked hard because I thought I was in downtown Tokyo.

"There's nothing but…o-o-oriental women up here," I slurred.

Honestly, I think this must have been the first time I had ever been exposed to Asian women. In Lake Charles, all we had were black and white people. I don't think we even had any Chinese restaurants. These women were hot, but they didn't really make me want to part with any of my yen. We walked up the next flight of stairs. Frank had saved the best for last.

"Jack…pot," I announced, out of breath.

There were beautiful black women of all shades everywhere. There were African honeybees, British babes, Caribbean cuties, and just plain old corn-fed, big-thighed "black guhls."

"I'ma meet y'all downstairs," Moore said, walking into a nearby room. He greeted the slim beauty standing outside it like they were old friends.

"Uh, yeah, me too," Frank said, disappearing down the dimly lit hall.

"Hey, where y'all…going?" I asked, my voice trailing off.

There I was, alone in the middle of a dark hallway, drunk, with a pocketful of money, and surrounded by dozens of beautiful hookers who wanted me…I mean, wanted my money. Me? I wanted my mommy.

"Hey, handsome," a voice purred from the darkness. It had such a lovely lilt to it. "Over here."

I cautiously turned.

"Come closer," she beckoned.

I inched forward and the closer I got to her, the more breath was sucked out of my lungs.

*Oh my God*, I thought, my eye sockets popping. She couldn't have been more than twenty and was wearing a red two-piece bra and G-string set—and wearing them very, very well. I immediately began thinking of our life together. I couldn't wait to get her a green card.

"Ya' like wah cha see?" she asked, a hint of the Caribbean in her accent.

"Hi," I said, hypnotized, waving my right hand.

She threw her head back and laughed. "What cha g'won do, bwoy?"

"Hi," I said, waving again.

She said her name was Cherry and she had been waiting all day for me and that this was her first day on the job and I was her very first customer and that I was the most handsome man she had ever seen—and as I stood there gazing at her, she ran her hands all over my chest and stomach, then squeezed my manhood and said I was the biggest ever.

And I believed her.

"Ya wan' come inside?" she asked. Who ever said there was no such thing as a dumb question?

Once the door closed behind me, I became really nervous. It sounded like cell bars clanking shut. I don't know if the tequila goggles I had been wearing had worn off or what, but she didn't look so hot anymore.

What have I gotten myself into?

Once we were inside, Cherry was all business. She deftly unhooked her bra and wiggled out of her thong. It was "$30 dollars for this," "$75 for that," "$100 if I wanted to use that thing on the dresser, batteries extra."

I swallowed hard. "Could we just talk?"

"Ya' nervous, mon?" she asked.

I made a hard face then puffed out my chest all big and bold, and then squeaked, "Yes."

Then, she let the games begin. While Cherry reached for my zipper, I sucked in my stomach and backed away. She then tried to hug me... I ducked and dodged her. Cherry made an attempt to kiss me, but I flinched and scrunched up my face. After nearly a minute of this, she had me cornered. I threw my hands up.

"Look," I tried to explain. "I've never done this before."

Cherry stuck out her abnormally long tongue out and wiggled the tip. Clearly, she had done this before.

"Tell me about yourself," I asked, fending off her advances. "Where are you from?"

Cherry faked left, I went right, then "bam!" She pinned me against the door and began licking my neck.

"Awww God," I cringed, as the hot saliva burned a hole in my Adam's apple. It felt like a German shepherd was licking me. Her breath smelled like ass, but more likely balls. I pushed her off and threw a wad of bills on the dresser.

"That should cover the bill," I said before dashing back to the bar. I felt dirty, and only numerous glasses of tequila could cleanse me.

Later on downstairs, I ran into Frank and Moore.

"How was your girl?" Frank asked.

I cleared my throat. "Oh, she was an animal."

**M**Y FIRST SIX MONTHS IN THE ARMY, I SPENT SO MUCH TIME IN A tent, I thought I had mistakenly joined the Boy Scouts.

As a 13 Foxtrot, otherwise known as a forward observer, I was constantly in the woods on field maneuvers observing or participating in war games, some lasting as long as sixty days. It didn't matter if it was in sunshine, rain, or a blizzard. I quickly came to the conclusion that if you're not a runaway slave or an escapee from a chain gang, there is really no good reason to be sludging through the forest for any longer than a week.

I should also note that being "in the field" was especially hard on military marriages. How can you sustain a relationship when your mate was away for months at a time? The Army divorce rate was nearly fifty percent. It wasn't uncommon for a married soldier to come home early from maneuvers only to find his wife getting maneuvered.

There were three main areas in Germany where the Army sent its soldiers to train en masse. One was Grafenwoehr, a massive gunnery range surrounded by thick forests and steep hills. The sounds of war could be heard all day and night. We trained for every wartime contingency—except one.

"Watch out for the pigs," Corporal King had warned me. I should have known something was up the way he grinned when he warned me. But as usual, I ignored his advice and walked off into the woods to relieve myself. Moments later, I came crashing back through the brush, pants around my ankles, a mean pack of wild boars nipping at my ass.

The second area where we trained was in Wildflecken, a craggy expanse of woods and deep ravines where we practiced shooting the .60 caliber machine gun. We hated going to Wildflecken because no matter the season, the forecast was always for snow. The area could be in the middle of a summer heat wave but the moment we got off the trucks, a nor'easter would hit. We did everything in the snow—trained, ate, even bathed. Snowballs had a different meaning in Wildflecken.

Grafenwoehr and Wildflecken were bad but the worst, wettest, muddiest, and miserablest place ever to train was in the town of Hohenfels. I nearly froze to death there. It happened on the coldest day I ever experienced, 20 degrees below zero, and the snow was ankle deep. My team and I were traveling in a specially equipped new vehicle called a FIST-V, short for fire support vehicle, a thirteen-ton piece of high technology. The FIST-V had laser optics and a state-of-the-art computer system that linked it with a global positioning system. It was advanced. I also didn't know how to work any of it. I was on a new team by then. It was myself, Sergeant Wayne, Private First Class Terry Maxwell (our driver) from Miami, Private Mike Wilson from Virginia Beach, and Specialist 4 Anderson, (one of those rare times he's wasn't out on sick call). Anderson and Sergeant Wayne were arguing over directions. We were in the middle of REFORGER, the most important war game of the year. This was a Europe-wide event with tens of thousands of troops involved. Time was running out and we had to link up with a unit we were supporting. The two were like an old couple arguing. Exasperated, Sergeant Wayne threw down the map.

"Okay, Anderson, we'll go your way."

Wilson and I looked at each other skeptically. Anderson was never right, so why Sergeant Wayne would trust his judgment was beyond us. I had been in the Army less than two years and Anderson had nearly ten years in and we were almost the same rank. Wilson and I tried to speak up but were shot down. What could we do? Anderson outranked us.

"Make a right, here," he barked to Maxwell.

"But And—?" Maxwell attempted to say.

Anderson eyed him hard and pulled rank. "Make a goddamn right, private."

Maxwell swerved and made a right—right into a massive sinkhole that could have swallowed a woolly mammoth.

"What the fu—?" Black yelled, spilling hot coffee all over us. We were bounced around like ping pong balls. Anderson landed on top of Wayne and Wilson was upside down in the back of the vehicle. I nearly bit my tongue in half. Equipment was tossed all over the inside of the FIST-V. I thought a stray howitzer round had hit us. As we got our bearings, Wayne struggled to push open the hatch.

He was seething. "I don't friggin' believe this."

One by one we peeked outside like astronauts emerging from a rocket on a strange planet. None of us could believe we what saw. We were stuck in the LaBrea Tar Pit of potholes. The front end of our $15 million dollar FIST-V was covered in mud. I'm glad we were on a dry-fire mission, because Wayne was reaching for his M16. We had to restrain him from killing Anderson. We had more pressing concerns.

Our vehicle was slowly sinking deeper into the mud. And it started snowing again. And it was freezing outside. And the engine went dead. And it was getting dark.

"Base, this is Alpha Bravo, come in," I said squeezing the radio's handset. And then the radio went dead.

We all looked at Wayne. He wrapped a scarf around his thick neck. "Y'all better bundle up."

Two hours later, the metal FIST-V had turned into a giant refrigerator, and we were like hanging sides of beef. I had dreamed of dying a warrior's death on a faraway battlefield, weapon in hand, dead enemies stacked at my feet. Not this way, in a mud puddle surrounded by stinking feet.

Finally, after hours of static, the radio crackled to life. I gave headquarters our position, but because of the snow falling, a rescue wouldn't come until the next morning. That meant we were in for a long, cold night.

I was hungrier than a hyena, but we had no food. The main reason we were linking up with our unit was to get resupplied. We began to turn on each other. Anderson had lied, saying he was going outside to pee, but we caught him eating a frozen Snickers bar. He nearly lost his life over a handful of nougat. We were eventually rescued a day and a half later, but that night we made a pact: If it came to it, the first person that would be eaten would be Anderson.

**B**AM! BAM! BAM! CAME THE KNOCK AT MY BARRACKS DOOR. I jumped up, hiding the latest issue of *Blacktail* under my pillow. It was Private Jordan, my company commander's hayseed orderly.

"Cap'n Hanes wanna see y'all," he said.

"Yassir," I mocked.

I wondered what the captain could want. He never called individual soldiers unless it was for something big. I stroked my chin. Well, I have been doing great lately, I had to admit to myself. I must have impressed him. Maybe the captain wanted to give me a promotion, a medal for bravery? Maybe he had an invitation for me to join the elite Rangers?

I marched right into Captain Hanes's office, snapped to attention, and saluted. "Private First Class Harmon reporting as ordered...sir."

Captain Hanes got up from behind his desk, slowly walked over to me, then looked me in the eye.

"Why haven't you been calling your mother?"

Call my momma?

My mother had called The Dime to drop a dime on me. She had reached the captain, wanting to know why the Army wouldn't let her son call home. It wasn't that the Army wouldn't let me call home. It was just too damn expensive to call home—something like twenty dollars for only a few minutes. That was drinking money. So, mainly, I wrote letters.

"When was the last time you went home on leave?" the captain asked.

"Never," I answered.

I had been in Germany for eighteen months and had never been back home. Captain Hanes ordered me to take leave.

I had to admit I was excited about going home. I especially wanted to see three girls—Tonia, Vicky, and Melissa. Their scantily clad pictures and steamy love letters were taped all over my wall locker. I had to keep it padlocked so my buddies wouldn't steal the photos.

I had dated each of these girls at different times during high school, but while I was overseas I eagerly awaited their perfume-spritzed letters. They wrote me nearly every week. Ah, the lies of young love. Melissa wrote that she thought we'd make a cute baby, Tonia said she wanted to have my baby, and Vicky was so damn fine, I wanted to have her baby.

It was lonely as hell in Germany. There were 17,000 people on base and of those, 14,000 had testicles. I'd say there were maybe 300 black women to choose from, with half of them being married. But that didn't matter, because women had it made. Young horny soldiers happily spent their entire checks on girls without ever having a chance at sex with them. I knew one girl who told me that she deposited every one of her own Army paychecks and never made a withdrawal. I believed her, too, because she damn sure deposited one of mine. It was one of the worst investments I ever made.

"*Jet* magazine may have its Beauty of the Week," I explained to my roommates at the time, Devlin and Wilson, as I marveled at the photos of Tonia, Vicky, and Melissa. "But I got Booties of the Week."

"Quit lying," Devlin cracked. "Those pictures came with that new wallet you got for Christmas."

Wilson doubled over with laughter.

"I know you ain't giggling," I replied. "Especially with that poster of your big-ass girlfriend Detray on your wall, looking like Gerald Levert with a perm." It was Devlin's turn to crack up. Private First Class Devlin was from the South Bronx and would never let you forget it.

"The Bronx is in the house!" he'd often yell on the dance floor.

He was always decked out in the latest hip-hop gear, wearing Kangol hats and huge gold rope necklaces around his neck. He was also, as they say in the boxing world, very nice with his hands. He knocked out dudes all over base. Devlin also had the nerves of a cat burglar. He would casually walk into the PX and just grab a typewriter or stereo off the shelf and walk right out of the store. Another technique of his would be to go into a clothing store wearing a baggy jogging suit. Next, he'd take a few suits into a dressing room, put on a full suit, then put the jogging attire back on and walk out of the store.

"How can you just waltz right out of the door like that?" I asked, stunned by his boldness.

Devlin shrugged. "No one would ever expect a person to do that, that's how."

Private Wilson was from Virginia Beach. Wilson was skinny, but his foot speed was legendary. One afternoon he was in the 400-meter final at a battalion track meet and wasn't paying attention when the starter pistol fired. He stood there looking crazy while the all the runners took off. He looked at us like, *What do I do?*

"Run, fool!" we yelled.

He took off like the cops were chasing him. In no time flat, he caught up with them, and we all stood there slack-jawed as he blew by the leader to win the race.

Those were my two main friends in Germany. They were both jealous that I was getting to go home on leave, and they envied the sexual harassment I was hoping to receive.

"I'm 'bout to be the Black Jack Tripper," I bragged.

Devlin rolled his eyes. "My ass. You gon' be in your momma's bathroom doing the cocoa butter five-knuckle shuffle."

"Yeah," Wilson chimed in. "Forget Bruce Lee, you gon' have the real 'Fists of Fury.'"

My comrades were misguided. I had every intention of sexin' like a felon fresh outta jail. I had been in Germany for more than a year and a half, so you can imagine how much I was looking forward to a conjugal visit. In my mind, I was going home for an entire month of raw, butt-naked sex. I was going to surprise my girls, I decided. They had no idea I was coming home.

The plane ride from Germany was twelve hours, so I had plenty of time to plan my itinerary once I got to Guinn Street. My first stop would be Victoria's. Her last name was King and it fit her well, because I worshipped her like royalty.

Pops had taken one look at her and said, "Dat girl is built like a brick shithouse."

Vicky was 5'9" and shaped like an hourglass, but with a long greasy Jheri-curl. Every time we'd kiss, the side of my face would look like I'd just eaten a three-piece dinner from Popeye's.

Tonia would be the next stop on the hit parade. Now, she and I went *way* back. I first met Tonia in Mrs. Reagan's second-grade class. Our desks were side by side and had our names taped on them. One day, I sat in Tonia's seat and Donald Glodd, future class clown, yelled out "Ooh, Byron likes Tonia." But Tonia moved away after that year, and I didn't see her again until my junior year in high school at a football game. She was with my best friend Dale's girlfriend. When I saw her, I couldn't believe my eyes. Tonia's hair was pulled back like the singer Sade's and she had on a tight pair of Chic no-pocket jeans. A girl had to have a remarkable posterior to sport Chic no-pockets.

"Damn," I elbowed Dale. "She got more curves than I-10. Who is that?"

Dale thought for a second. "I think her name is Tonia."

A huge smile crossed my face. "I know that girl!"

I casually walked over to her and said, "Hello—where are my Now and Laters?"

"Excuse me?" she snapped. Tonia had on that 'you better get out my face with that' look that black women, if they didn't invent it, have certainly perfected.

I smiled. "Ten years ago I gave you a whole pack of grape Now and Laters, and you said you'd buy me some later. Well…it's later."

Tonia squinted, trying to recognize me. "Byron?" We dated for a good part of that next year.

I met Melissa in the summer of 1986 on a hot Sunday night at Skate City Roller Rink. She looked so sweet and beautiful standing there all by herself, like the last box of Fruity Pebbles on a grocery store shelf.

I nudged my friend Donavan. "Who is that?"

"I don't know." He answered. "But if I had to guess, a woman who looks like she wouldn't want yo' broke ass."

I mumbled "Whatever" and walked in her direction. When I reached her, I leaned close and whispered, "If I told you that you had a beautiful body, would you hold it against me?"

She just stared at me, popping her bubblegum, one hand perched sassily on one of her hips.

"Wasn't cute, huh?" I asked.

She rolled her pretty brown eyes. "Not even close."

At that moment, the DJ started spinning Cheryl Lynn's "Got to Be Real."

"Would you like to dance?" I asked.

She shook her head no.

My face fell. "C'mon, don't diss me. All my boys are watching us. *Puhleeze?*"

I began dancing the "Robot" in front of her.

"C'mon…crazy boy." She grabbed my arm and led me to the dance floor.

We danced for two songs—until Luther Vandross's "If Only for One Night" came on.

I smiled. *Thank you, God.*

Melissa began walking away, but I grabbed her hand. "C'mon, one dance?"

"I don't slow-dance with strangers," she snarled, pushing my hand away.

I cleared my throat. "Well then, allow me to introduce myself, my name is Byron, and don't worry—I'm a Christian."

Melissa laughed and slid into my arms. While the DJ spun "If Only for One Night," I was thinking, If only for about one minute.

"Do you have a boyfriend?" I whispered in her ear.

She nodded yes.

"Why'd he let a fine woman like you come out here all by yourself?"

"He didn't," she explained. "He's here."

*Uh oh*, I thought, nervously looking over her shoulder. I tried to sound casual. "Oh really? Why aren't you two dancing?"

"Oh, he can't come inside the skating rink. They banned him."

"Wwwhy?" I stuttered.

Melissa popped her bubblegum. "Cuz he always be fighting and stuff."

It always amazes me how women can describe their crazy boyfriends in such a nonchalant voice.

"Who's your boyfriend?

"They call him Boogie," she said.

I was slow dancing with the girlfriend of the craziest dude at my high school. Boogie fought all the time. As soon as the song ended, I said, "Goodbye, good luck, have a nice life, and I hope Boogie doesn't kill you."

After that, I saw Melissa out sporadically. We'd speak for a hot minute and go on our way until one night at the Budweiser Superfest. Maze and Frankie Beverly were about to perform, and I was hurrying back to my seat when she called my name. After scanning the vicinity for the possibility of "Boogie Beatdown," I walked over. That's when Melissa whispered the three magic words I dreamed of hearing her say in my ear: "Boogie's in jail."

"Excuse me. Wake up, sir," the flight attendant said, tapping my shoulder, "We're in Lake Charles."

I was home and in no time at all I was back on Guinn Street. It was hot in Louisiana at that time of the year. Hell, it was hot at any time of the year in Louisiana. All I wanted to do was kiss my mother, give Pops a pound, and then get naked with Vicky, Tonia, and Melissa. But I had to eat first—Southern-fried, clogged arteries style. My mom cooked all my favorite dishes, like BBQ chicken and ribs, neck-bones, red beans and rice, potato salad, cornbread dressing, and homemade biscuits. In Germany, we mostly ate Army rations called MREs, for "Meals Ready-to-Eat." To me, it stood for "Meals Rejected by Ethiopians."

After eating, I called Vicky. Her younger sister informed me that she was at work. Vicky worked as a waitress at a restaurant by the beach. I borrowed Pops's van to go see her. Vicky's green Pacer was parked outside.

"I see you still got that ass," I called to the nice-looking girl I saw as I walked in. But when the ass turned around, it wasn't Vicky's—it was the manager's.

"Excuse me—what did you say?"

"Oh, pardon me, Miss," I said, weakly. "I said, 'Be still, or you'll knock over that glass.'"

The manager seemed surprised that I wanted to see Vicky. I waited while she went to get her. When Vicky walked out, I nearly had a coronary. Vicky had gained at least 75 pounds.

Noticing my astonishment, she admitted, "I know. I'm a lil' heavier than I used to be."

No, I was thinking. A floor-model TV is heavy. Your ass is ginormous. But I was tactful. "You ain't that big, baby," I said, all the while looking at my watch.

Vicky smiled. "I'm so happy to see you, Byron. I'm 'bout to get off, can you follow me home?"

I was so dazed, I think I mumbled, "Yeah, sure, no problem."

She got into her car. She turned right. I turned left. I'm ashamed to say I haven't seen her since.

I immediately went off in search of Tonia. She worked at the McDonald's on Broad Street. I saw her car as soon as I walked under the Golden Arches.

Tonia was big-time now, a shift manager and was still fine as frog's hair.

"Hellooo baby cakes!" I announced flamboyantly.

Tonia stared at me, frozen.

It's never a good sign when the first thing a woman who hasn't seen you in nearly two years does is clear her throat. "Um, hey Byron, why didn't you tell me you were um, coming home?"

I tried my best to ignore my bullshit detector, because I just knew lightning couldn't strike twice in one day.

I leaned on the counter. "What time do you get off?"

Tonia got real professional. "My official off time is 11 pm, but uh, we can't hook up tonight."

"What do you mean, can't?"

"Can I get a rain check?" She fake-smiled while batting her long lovely eyelashes.

Rain check? It was about to start storming. "I haven't seen you in this long and I'm getting a goddamn rain check?"

The customers in line grew really quiet. A goofy looking coworker came to the rescue. "Gotta problem, Tonia?"

I rolled my eyes. "Hey fry guy? Go change the grease or something."

Tonia waved him off. "Can you calm down, please?"

"I ain't calming down," I exploded. "These people don't know me." Actually two of the people in line did know me—and they were laughing. Thank God YouTube wasn't around then.

"Who are you screwing?" I asked.

"Byron, please."

"Who in the hell are you seeing?"

She took a deep breath and came clean. "Darrel Daniels. Darrel Daniels and I are back together."

I reached across the counter to choke her, but she was too far away. "Darrel Daniels?" The name tasted rancid.

"Yes," she sighed.

Damn, I thought. Why couldn't it have been anybody else but Darrel Daniels? I mean, *Darrel Daniels*? If there was one dude in the world that I hated, it was Darrel Daniels. I'd rather it had been my brother Andre than Darrel Daniels.

I lost control and started ranting like a diva. "What about those letters and all that talk about you wanting to have my baby?"

Tonia just shrugged her shoulders.

"Screw it," I sighed, looking up at the menu. "Gimme a number two. And don't be stingy with the fries."

Two strikes in one day? I was a wreck by the time I arrived at Melissa's. Her mother hugged and kissed me like I was coming home from a war. Melissa's mother was beautiful, and she always seemed to have a special place in her heart for me. Maybe it was because I was the only boyfriend Melissa had ever had that she didn't have to pass through a metal detector to visit.

"Melissa?" her mother yelled up the stairs. "You got a handsome visitor."

Handsome? Her mother sure knew what to say to a young man. I gave her the bouquet of flowers I was going to give to Melissa. I closed my eyes and listened to Melissa walk down the creaky stairs. The creaks sounded heavy.

"Oh my God, Byron!" Melissa screamed. "What are you doing here? You didn't call me or nothing, boy."

I slowly opened my eyes then just as slowly closed them. I opened them again and shook my head. No

Melissa was pregnant. Very. Speechless, I pointed to her stomach and looked at her mother like, *What the f...?* Melissa's mother looked at me like, *She didn't tell you? and* then hurriedly walked out of the room.

Melissa eyes avoided mine. "Byron, I...I don't know what to say. I'm sorry."

Not as sorry as I was. I felt like somebody punched me in the gut. "Who's the daddy?"

She looked down and rubbed her bulging belly. "Boogie."

I turned around and walked out of the door. I wanted to cry. I had waited nearly two years for this? It wasn't fair. I lost a lot of myself that day. I had just lost the loves of my life—all three of them—in a few hours' time.

I was so upset that in my weakened emotional state, I smoked a joint. I drove back to Guinn Street in a daze. I was headed to the bathroom when my mother asked, "Are you glad to be back home?"

"Absolutely," I lied. "By the way, do we have any cocoa butter?"

**A**FTER I LEFT LAKE CHARLES TO COME BACK FROM LEAVE, I vowed never to return. The trip traumatized me. I didn't know whether I was coming or going. My plan, to the extent I had one, was to re-enlist and live in Germany for the rest of my life.

The day after I returned was uneventful. So when my unit had its last formation of the day, I didn't think anything of it. It's normally a routine gathering in which Top, otherwise known as the first sergeant and the boss of all the enlisted soldiers, addresses the soldiers and talks about the next day's schedule. Formations were normally short and sweet, but this one dragged. We were getting antsy. It was chow time. Top then turned the formation over to Sergeant Wayne, who ran up front and took off his hat. We stole wary glances at each other.

"What this?" Devlin whispered out of the corner of his mouth.

I shook my head. "If he's involved, it can't be good."

"Look at that head," someone in the back mumbled. Indeed, Sergeant Wayne was cranially endowed.

"Troops," he snarled, then cited some gibberish about Army regulations and policies, but all I heard was the word *urinalysis*.

"A piss test?" I was stunned.

Wayne placed tiny pieces of paper with letters of the alphabet written on them in his hat. If your last name began with any of the letters, it was tinkle-time. My heart leaped into my throat. I was in big trouble. How could they have a urinalysis on the day after I came back off leave? One didn't have to be Woodward and Bernstein to figure this one out. I silently cursed Wayne. This had his Rasputin-like fingerprints all over it.

Wayne would have made a great soap opera villain. He was in charge of all the stuff that could get a soldier in trouble. He handled the urinalysis, the fitness exams, and oversaw all alcohol-related incidents. He was in short, a Richard, which was Army longhand for dick. He tried to screw me every chance he got, but I was always able to outsmart him.

We were constantly at war. Once, he nearly had me locked up after a sensitive codebook went missing, a codebook that he had signed for. I think he was jealous of me. I was definitely one of the young guns to watch. All of the other sergeants wanted me on their teams and he couldn't take it, so he took it out on me by always trying to embarrass me. I really hated him. But this was to be his *coup de grace*. A hot piss test would get me kicked out of the Army. I know I was wrong to get high, but did I deserve a dishonorable discharge? And besides—how did he know?

I stood there shaking with fear while Wayne called out a few initials, but mine wasn't one of them. Maybe he'd look out for me after all. Then...

"H," Wayne said with relish. "If your last name begins with H, go upstairs."

I stared icicles at him. He didn't even look my way.

"And the final initial...X," I heard him call out, as I stepped out of formation. That's when I knew it was a conspiracy. X? We didn't have any Chinese soldiers in our unit.

By the time I got upstairs, I was as nervous as R. Kelly at a Girl Scout convention. Fat beads of sweat slid down my forehead. I prayed.

*Lord, I promise you that if you get me outta this...*

I lingered as long as I could without looking too suspicious. I was the last person in a line of nearly thirty soldiers waiting on Wayne. I watched from a nearby window as my friends went to eat chow. They looked so happy. I felt like the sick kid who couldn't go out to play. But something was odd. Wayne wasn't heading upstairs. He was walking to the parking lot. He got in his Volvo and left.

Where is he going?

Whatever, I had made up my mind to plead the fifth. I decided that I wasn't going to pee. My heart was about to explode. My face was a mask of ash. I didn't care how long I had to stay upstairs, I wasn't giving up the goods, even if they tortured me.

*Lord, just gimme a sign to let me know you hear me.*

Then I heard a loud, thunderous voice. It was majestic and resounding.

"All right, shitbirds, line up."

OK—not the voice of God, but still a good sign.

The staff sergeant who was going to administer the test was an old, crusty, burned-out Vietnam veteran named Whitehead. He had been in the Army more than twenty years and was only a staff sergeant. It was safe to say he wasn't that motivated. Whitehead had a victim mentality, and that day he was feeling especially persecuted.

"I can't believe they got me doing this crap," he growled. "I'm going on leave this afternoon."

One by one, soldiers lined up and submitted their samples, all except for me. I was the last man standing.

"Sorry, Sarge," I shrugged. "I can't pee."

"What?" he said, exasperated.

"Sorry. I took a leak right before formation."

He looked at his old Timex. "Geez Louise. Drink some water or something."

We waited and waited and waited. Then, after waiting, we waited some more. I was willing to wait until the Second Coming. Old Sarge wasn't.

"Get outta my face, Harmon," he ordered. "I have to catch a plane."

He didn't have to tell me twice. I made a quick exit.

"Don't tell nobody," he warned.

*Please.* I would never snitch. Not unless it would get me out of trouble.

After that episode, I knew I had to get out of Germany. Wayne had re-enlisted for four more years, and there was no way I was sticking around for Richard to stick it to me.

The third Monday of January 1990 was a doubly special day for me. It was Dr. Martin Luther King, Jr.'s birthday, and it was the day I received my transfer orders.

"Free at last…free at last," I sang, waving the orders in the air. "Thank God Almighty, I'm free from Sergeant Wayne's ass at last."

But freedom came with a high price tag. I was being transferred to Kansas—Ft. Riley to be exact, home of the First Infantry Division, aka the Big Red One. It was one of the most famous and most decorated divisions in the history of the Army. But it was still in Kansas. My buddies didn't know whether to congratulate me or offer condolences.

"Where in the hell is Kansas?" I asked as they crowded into my room to pay their respects.

Private Elliott, a brother from Brooklyn, shook his head. "I think it's in Iowa."

The room fell silent. Private Elliott wasn't the sharpest knife in the drawer. The answers he sometimes blurted out were legendary. We'd even given them a name, "Elliottisms." To the eternal shame of us all, his most famous one was uttered in front of a dozen white officers.

"What did you study in college?" He asked Lieutenant Shiry, a snobbish West Point graduate who was also our platoon leader.

"Economics," Lt. Shiry answered.

Elliott sucked his teeth. "Personally, I don't give a damn about the Russians."

Elliott had the worst luck, too. In the span of a few weeks he received a DUI while riding a bicycle and was caught on camera pocketing hundreds of dollars after an ATM malfunctioned, spitting out money at him like a fountain. I was going to miss Elliott. When all of my friends had left the room, I looked at my orders and sighed. What am I going to do in Kansas?

If only I could have been stronger. According to my enlistment contract, I was actually due to be discharged in May 1990. However, I was so sick of Wayne that I extended my tour by eight months just to leave Germany early. That was the last time I signed a contract without a lawyer.

I didn't get a chance to have a big going-away party because my unit was away at "Winter Warrior," a major war game exercise conducted in the snow. I thanked God that I didn't have to deal with that. I was sick of the snow. A week later, I was in Ft. Riley, Kansas, up to my knees in guess what? Snow.

I knew I was in for a different experience when I checked in. The old white-haired sergeant on duty looked at my spit-shined boots and starched BDUs and shook his head.

"You don't have to do that here," he laughed, while I signed my name on the clipboard.

In Germany, it was standard procedure to be spit-and-polished. You couldn't have one lace untied or button unbuttoned, not with Wayne's fashion brigade lurking in the shadows. Germany was about being a professional-looking, well-trained soldier. We trained hard and had a grueling daily fitness regimen. We had to, because in spite of how Private Elliott felt, we did give a damn about the Russians. We were, after all, still in a Cold War. However, back in the States, it was a different story.

My unit on Ft. Riley was called the first of the fifth field artillery (1/5FA), aka "The Nickel." Life in The Nickel was like the movie *Stripes.* Our first sergeant, Top Hall, was the spitting image of Jed Clampett from *The Beverly Hillbillies,* and just as old. We rarely trained and never went on maneuvers—even physical training was voluntary. Our motto was, "We do less before 5 pm than most soldiers do all day."

I had three new roommates, all of them white. Now, that was not a problem. The problem, it turned out, was that one of them was a neo-Nazi skinhead. Another was the son of a Texas Grand Wizard of the KKK. The last was a devil worshiper.

This has to be a mistake, I thought.

When I walked in, the stereo was cranked to full volume blasting Black Sabbath or Led Zeppelin or some other group dedicated to helping angry white youth get even angrier. On the wall was displayed a gigantic Confederate rebel flag. On a nearby shelf was a replica of a Nazi storm trooper helmet. An open copy of *The Satanic Bible* lay on one of the beds— my new bed.

I don't care how the recruiting posters portray it: the Army can be a really racist environment. Ethnic groups pretty much congregated together, so it was only natural that we developed suspicions of each other. At one point while in Germany, I became very paranoid. Everything became a conspiracy to keep black people down. I joined the new Black Panther Party, and we'd have late-night meetings to discuss black history and radical philosophies. I was reading incendiary literature like *Soul on Ice* and *Soledad Brother.* For a time, I even contemplated converting to Islam.

Needless to say, all conversation ceased when I walked into the room. I went over to the empty bunk and picked up *The Satanic Bible* and gave it to Ozzy Osbourne, Jr.

I then threw my duffle bag on the bed and began unpacking and thinking about how I was going to go AWOL. After a few minutes, I couldn't take it anymore.

"Yo!" I yelled over the screeching guitar riffs and motioned for the music to be turned down.

The neo-Nazi rolled his eyes and turned it down just a notch. I looked at the Grand Wizard's son and said, "You gon' have to take down that flag."

He gave me the finger. "I ain't taking jack down. You're the new guy."

They all laughed at that line, but I had something for them. I took off my jacket and rolled up my sleeves so they could see my Black Panther tattoo. Then I placed on the wall some of my own mementoes that were dear to me. Over my bed, I put up a poster showing Malcolm X shaking hands with Dr. Martin Luther King, Jr.

"You some kind of troublemaker?" asked the Grand Wizard's son.

I ignored him and taped a red, black, and green Jamaican flag that had a picture of Bob Marley on it to the wall. Out of my duffle bag, I pulled out a copy of the book *The Making of the White Man* and placed it on my nightstand. We now had our own cold war—the white supremacists versus the Panthers. Funny thing happened, though: after a few weeks, we all got along fine and would even have long philosophical discussions about race and society. Sure, they were all still stupid, asshole bigots, but if the Army says you have to live together, then what can you do? But later still, after getting into a fistfight with the devil worshiper, who then tried to stab me with some weirdly shaped sword, I didn't feel safe sleeping there. I moved into a trailer off base.

In Kansas, I fell apart fast, and the disciplined soldier I'd been in Germany became a memory. At Ft. Riley, I became an alcoholic. I was drunk six nights of the week. I'd warm up with two forties of Old English 800, then chase that with a sixteen-ounce bottle of Cisco, a cheap ghetto wine also known as liquid crack. Once inside a nightclub, I would promptly order two Long Island Iced Teas and a Heineken. I would then proceed to spend the next couple of hours reenacting classic dance moves from *Soul Train*. Some mornings I would awaken in nearby towns, not knowing how I got there or the name of the woman I was in bed with.

In hindsight, I was pitiful. Most of the time I would drag myself in with just enough time to make the morning formation. My buddies and I would be standing in line reeking of cheap liquor and the smell of even cheaper women. The nightclubs on and around base were infamous. There was The Alibi. So many people would be packed in there on a Saturday night, it was the perfect place to get one. On Friday nights we'd hang out at The Polo Club, aptly named because most of the Army women in there looked like horses. Other nights, you could find us at the VFW, also known as Very Fat Women. Once, a drunken eighty-year-old woman hit on me. She would not take no for an answer.

"C'mon…young buck," she slurred. "Just one dance."

I stared at her in utter disbelief. "You must be out of your mind, Grandma."

Grandma was unfazed. She actually started dancing seductively in front of me! She was licking her lips and vogueing like Madonna. I cringed. For Chrissakes, she was all gums. Meanwhile, my buddies were at the bar crying with laughter.

I laughed and looked around for the hidden camera. "This is a joke, right?"

Grandma was smiling, but she was not joking. She slid her hand in mine but I jerked it away and ran out of the club.

Some days I felt guilty, though, as if I were stealing money from the government. This guilt was fleeting, however, thanks to the influence of my two partners in crime. Their nicknames were KD and Drew. They called me Harmnice (for some reason, I always got the dumb nickname).

Kevin D. Edwards was a 6'3" brother from New York who sported an Empire State Building-sized high-top fade and a sparkling gold tooth. He was a life-of-the party type and loved to announce my entrance to any bar we entered.

"Harm…nice!" he drawled, mimicking the exaggerated voice of a game show announcer. "Sounds so sweet gotta say it twice."

"Harm…nice!" I would respond on cue. I know. It was stupid, I know. But I was nineteen years old.

KD had pimp in his blood. He wielded a mystical power over the women in his life. They'd do anything for him. One time he had two dates show up in the lobby of the barracks at the same time. One was a tall, thick, cocoa-colored beauty named Pam. The other was a very light-skin hottie named Dell. The ladies had to be separated to keep from clawing each other while KD came down. We all gathered around, anxious to witness the scene.

"What KD gon' do?" someone asked.

No one knew for sure. Some guys placed bets. When he entered the lobby, KD was calm as he surveyed the volatile situation.

"Hmm," he rubbed his chin for a few seconds.

The ladies cut their eyes at him like, "Well?"

KD grinned, gold tooth glinting in the light. "I'll take you."

Dell and him left together arm in arm. Pam stood there seething with her hands on her hips, but the very next day, she was the lucky woman in KD's room. I don't know how KD pulled it off.

Andrew Kemp was from Michigan, and was cooler than the other side of the pillow. The Fonz didn't have a thing on Drew. He was handsome and short, maybe 5'5", with a mass of curly hair on top and faded on the sides. I'd often see him in the mirror spritzing on curl activator.

"Whatcha doing, Drew?" I asked.

He smiled. "Spraying my juices and berries."

He also had a drinking problem—he couldn't. One beer would turn him into a raving lunatic.

"I ain't drunk," he'd slur and stumble, knocking over glasses and anything else on the bar. "Y'all always say I'm drunk. Why y'all say I'm drunk?"

Then he'd start crying. I can't count the times KD and I carried Drew home from The Alibi after he had passed out at a table or threw up on the dance floor. Yes, he threw up while dancing.

Those were crazy times. We were like a twister cutting a wide swath through the plains of Kansas. Maybe it was the total lack of discipline and structure in our unit that made us so reckless. We partied from Topeka to Wichita. Some weeknights, we even drove the two hours to Kansas City and still made it back for morning formation. To mask our exploits, we had chipped in together and rented a rusty two-bedroom doublewide trailer off base. It was raggedy, but it served our purpose. Using it as a base of operations, we'd have barbecues and drinking parties, Bacchanalian feasts rivaling anything ancient Rome ever put on.

Drugs were big in Kansas (I never had to worry about a piss test at Ft. Riley). Hell, we always had weed at the trailer. One time, our neighbors dropped a dime on us because of our loud music. When the cops banged on our trailer door, I nearly threw up with fear.

I steeled myself and took a deep breath before opening the door. "Yes, Officer, is there a problem?"

He stood there tall, corn-fed, and rednecked. "The loud music, can y'all make sure and keep that down?"

"Yes, sir," I said, trying to block his prying eye.

He left, and we let out the deepest sigh ever. If the cop had stepped inside the trailer, he would have noticed that sitting right behind the open door was a trash bag filled with marijuana. We tried our hands at being drug dealers, but wound up smoking our entire product.

Now, when I look back at that time, I shudder at what could have become of me. I routinely thank God for sparing me. We were playing a dangerous game. If we were caught, not only would we have been kicked out of the Army, we would have definitely gone to Leavenworth Penitentiary.

But someone stopped us dead in our tracks. It wasn't the cops, though. It was Saddam Hussein.

**M**ILITARY SECRETS ARE, BY DEFINITION, SECRET. THE ARMY HAS myriad levels of protocols, chains of command, and encryption techniques and codes to keep information under wraps. So with all of that sophisticated military communications technocrap, how come my unit found out it was going to war from CNN?

It was November of 1990 and the day of discovery began and ended like so many others. There were no omens or signs of impending doom. After the last formation, my buddies and I gathered in the barracks to watch TV and wait for the chow hall to open. I held court as my buddies sat wide-eyed, regaling them with tales of the Bayou Classic, a legendary football game that pitted Southern University versus Grambling.

The Bayou Classic is held in New Orleans on the Saturday after Thanksgiving and with more than 100,000 black people choking Bourbon Street, it is one of the biggest parties next to Mardi Gras.

"Thousands of college babes will be there," I boasted.

"I'm coming this year," KD said emphatically. "Ain't no way I'm missing out on all them broads."

"Me too," Drew said.

"Me three," Specialist Washington chimed in. Washington was a cool brother from South Carolina.

I laughed. "Let's rent a van and take everybody!"

I couldn't wait to take the fellas to New Orleans for this trip—at this point, only three weeks away. Bringing all my Army buddies home this way would be one of the biggest events of my life. It would also serve as a proper going-away party for me, since I was up for honorable discharge right before Christmas. I would finally be out of the Army. No more fatigues, no more "yassir boss" to nerdy officers, and no more shaving. I vowed to grow a Grizzly Adams beard when I got home. I was giddy at the thought. Just forty more days.

The thought of becoming a civilian again consumed nearly all of my waking thoughts. By now I'd become thoroughly disgusted with the Army way of life. I had bigger dreams than getting another stripe on my shoulder. Besides, the longer one stayed in the Army, the harder it was to adjust to civilian life. (It was similar to jail in that way, apparently.) I didn't want to be one of those brothers who came home from the Army still wearing a leisure suit while the rest of Black America was wearing Hugo Boss.

Our Bayou Classic planning session was interrupted by a news flash from Bernard Shaw, CNN's lead anchor.

"We have breaking news," his deep voice boomed. It was a rich, authoritarian baritone, perfect for announcing the apocalypse.

"Turn it up," I said to KD.

Bernard Shaw shuffled his pile of scripts for effect. "CNN has learned that the Big Red One division based in Ft. Riley, Kansas has been activated for deployment to the Middle East."

"Huh?" KD asked.

Drew looked at me with fear in his eyes. "What?"

"Did he say what I thought he said?" I asked, dazed. As if on cue, Bernard Shaw repeated the information.

"Deployed?" I joked. "More like screwed."

We were shocked—and awed. How could CNN know this? We had just come from formation. You'd think our superiors would have mentioned a little thing like the fact we were going to war. I gave my comrades a sympathetic face and patted KD on the back.

"That's a tough break, bro," I said with concern. "I'ma pray for y'all."

KG rolled his eyes. "What do you mean y'all? You coming too."

I violently shook my head. "Nuh-uh. I'm short forty days. I've turned in all my gear. It's back to the world for me."

"Damn," KD sighed, his head hung low. "You lucky."

Finally, I had some luck worth having.

A half-hour later, while we were eating chow, the base alarm sounded. We were ordered to report to our individual units.

"Now they gon' tell us," Drew said, stuffing the last bite from a slice of banana cake in his mouth.

As we gathered around the front of our building waiting for our colonel, I was paying my respects to the other, soon-to-depart soldiers.

"I hope y'all don't end up dearly departed soldiers," I snickered. "Hey Spears! You want me to stop by your momma's house and check on her while you're gone?"

Spears, a country boy from Arkansas who sported a Gumby haircut, flipped me the bird.

Unfazed, I turned to KD. "Make sure and leave me your black book."

Honestly, I felt truly sorry for my friends. The rumor was that Saddam Hussein would have no problem using gas and nerve agents on our troops. Plus, his fearsome Republican Guard was supposed to be one of the most deadly fighting forces in the world.

"Attention!" the sergeant major commanded, jolting us back to reality. Our colonel slowly walked to the front and unfolded a sheet of paper.

"Gentlemen," he said solemnly. "We are going to war."

For a moment his voice was drowned out by the hoots and hollers of some of the more Rambo-type soldiers. Let me observe that none of the soldiers yelling were African-American. I didn't care one way or another, because I knew I wasn't going anywhere but home. The colonel cleared his throat and the formation fell silent again.

"All transfers and discharges have been put on hold...indefinitely."

I immediately felt faint and my knees wobbled. "What did...what did he say?"

KD grinned. His gold tooth shone brilliantly in the afternoon sun. "He said yo' black ass is going to war."

Going to war? If the Gulf War had happened two years earlier, when I was a super trooper, I would have been ecstatic. Back then, I was in love with the Army way of life, and combat would have been the crowning achievement of my career. However, years of abuse by sadistic supervisors like Sergeant Wayne, the feeling that I was nothing but a pawn, and the effects of hard drinking and hard living had taken their toll on me. I no longer wanted to be all that I could be. Go to war? I wanted to go home.

**D**OG, WE ARE GOING TO DIE," KD MOANED.

I hated to admit it, but I concurred.

From the moment we received the deployment alert, the soldiers in my unit were in a panic. The reason? Half of us had forgotten how to do our jobs. Getting drunk daily—plus the fact that we never, ever trained—has a way of eroding one's skills. Therefore, we had to cram a year of training into three short weeks. The only thing I could remember from my earlier training was that the life expectancy of a forward observer in combat was nine seconds.

"Dog, we *are* going to die," I said to KD.

We left for the Middle East on Jesus's birthday. Adding in the layovers, the trip was an excruciating twenty-three hours long. The only bright spot about the flight were the flight attendants. The cute ladies were extra-nice to us, but in the kind of way that corrections officers are nice to inmates who are hours away from a lethal injection. We landed in Dhahran, a small port city on the Persian Gulf. The first thing I noticed about Saudi Arabia was how hot it was. It was Alabama-cotton-pickin' hot.

"I don't know how slaves did it," Drew said, wiping the sweat from his forehead.

I didn't know how we were going to do it. The airstrip was abuzz with activity. There was no doubt that we were going to war. Everywhere I turned I saw M1 Abrams tanks, Bradley infantry fighting vehicles and Black Hawk helicopters. I also saw a lot of soldiers—thousands of them. Right then and there, I knew there was no way that Saddam stood a chance.

We were quickly shuttled to buses that took us to the Khobar Towers, a massive housing complex that would years later be the sight of a terrorist attack that took the lives of nineteen Americans. The rooms didn't have any furniture, but they were air-conditioned, and in the oppressive Middle Eastern heat, that turned out to be an enormous blessing.

Until my boss, Sergeant First Class Allen, explained that our living arrangements were only temporary.

"We're going to the desert," he said.

I gave him a confused look. "But we're in the desert, Sarge."

He pointed off in the distance. "We're going to that desert."

A few days later, one of the strangest things that ever happened to me occurred while KD and I were walking around the complex, exploring and taking in the sights. The amount of activity in the complex was overwhelming. Thousands of soldiers from units all over the world were coming in and out of Khobar Towers. As KD and I joked, I saw a familiar face walking toward me.

"What the..?" I said, rapidly blinking my eyes. "I don't believe it."

KG stopped in his tracks, his eyes darting. "What? What?"

I pointed at a tall, dark, slim soldier walking with two very attractive female officers.

"I'll be damned," I smiled. "That dude looks just like my older brother Andre."

KD sucked his teeth. "You're crazy."

Maybe I was seeing a mirage. I was in the desert after all. But as the three soldiers came closer, I realized I wasn't crazy. It was my brother.

"Andre?" I asked.

He froze, recognition slowly forming on his face. "Byron?"

"Oh my God!" we said in unison. I was stunned. Andre and I stood there looking at each other like two, well, long-lost brothers.

See, shortly after I joined the Army, Andre joined the Army Reserves. I guess he couldn't deal with my parents on his own. After he finished boot camp, he moved to Baton Rouge to attend Southern University. When the buildup for the Gulf War began, his reserve unit, the 321st Material Management Company, or MMC, handled a lot of the ordering and moving of equipment to Saudi Arabia. My mother had told me he had been deployed, but I didn't know where. I certainly never expected to run into him in a war. I was the combat soldier. This was my turf. But once again,

Andre outdid me. While I was stuck as a Specialist E-4 in an artillery unit, Andre was a Sergeant E-5, and was assigned to a supply company that was fully stocked with one of the Army's most precious resources—women. At least 60 percent of his unit was made up of women, and not the old regular Army type of women, but fresh-faced college co-eds. This explained why Andre was strolling with two stunning lieutenants. I gave his colleagues the quick once over. I was impressed. I hugged my brother close.

"Boy, you a pimp," I whispered in his ear.

He was silent and just smiled that wicked smile of his. One thing about Andre, he never acknowledged the obvious.

"Lil Bro, I can't believe this," he said turning to his two friends. "This is my little brother, y'all!"

After we all were introduced, Andre dropped another bombshell on me. "Guess who else is here?"

My eyes got wide. "Who?"

"The Guidrys."

"Quit playing."

"I'm not. They live downtown."

This was too much. The Guidrys were a family who had lived around the corner from us on Guinn Street. We grew up with their kids, Denise and Daryl, who was Andre's best friend. The Guidrys were like second parents to us. Mr. Guidry was a petroleum engineer with Saudi Aramco, the state-owned national oil company of Saudi Arabia. The company's headquarters was in Dhahran. The Guidrys had lived there for years. Andre told me how every other day he'd visit them, and Mrs. Guidry would cook for him and his friends. The Guidrys were living large, too. One time they even threw a lavish party for my brother's unit.

"You have to come to their house," Andre said. "It's beautiful, and they are going to die when they see you."

I wanted to see them, too, not to mention sample some real down-home food. Almost all I had eaten since I'd been in country were MREs. There was just one problem standing in the way of my reunion. My unit was shipping out to the desert in a day and a half, and I knew my superiors would never let me leave the compound. I couldn't be trusted to come back.

"You have to try," Andre pressed me.

I sighed and shrugged. "Say a prayer for me."

God was on my side, because after a whole lot of explaining, begging, and promises that I'd bring back my captain some chocolate cake, they let me spend the night.

As we drove through downtown Dhahran, I was amazed at how much it resembled downtowns that one would find in America. There were strip malls and even fast-food restaurants. And the drivers, who all seemed to be behind the wheels of huge Mercedes Benzes, were complete lunatics. We almost wrecked three times. But I really wasn't prepared for Andre's new digs. His unit had commandeered a luxury hotel. There were two soldiers assigned to each room, and these were all equipped with a bathroom and cable television. They had use of the hotel swimming pool, plus a chef to cook their meals.

"Damn, Andre," I said, impressed. "All that's missing is the harem."

That's when he pointed out one of the many beautiful female soldiers sharing this oasis in the desert.

I bit my lip. "Oh my! She's in your unit?"

Andre nodded.

I was blown away. Andre's unit was on vacation, not at war. I was jealous of the soldiers doing belly flops and somersaults into the cool waters of the indoor swimming pool. The girls wore bikinis and sat giggling poolside in deck chairs. Some of the male soldiers were even decked out in thobes and tagiyahs, the traditional Arabic cotton garment and knitted skull cap. Meanwhile, I stood there looking like an extra in the movie *Platoon*.

After a brief tour we set out for the Guidrys' house, where they rolled out the red carpet. We took pictures and reminisced about the fun times on Guinn Street. Then we ate steak, drank Kool-Aid, and had chocolate cake for dessert. As I sat at the table thinking about what was in store for me, I couldn't help but feel like it was the Last Supper. We prayed together, and Mrs. Guidry gave me a beautiful pillow to go along with my ugly Army-issue sleeping bag.

On the way back to Khobar Towers, we stopped at a KFC so I could buy my friends some fast food. KD and the gang mobbed me when I walked in carrying a big bucket of fried chicken and biscuits.

The next day my unit shipped off to the real desert. I was awestruck at the endless miles of sand and rising waves of heat. I thought we had landed on Mars. I noticed one major problem as soon as I stepped off the truck.

"Yo, Sarge? Where are the bathrooms?"

He looked at me as if I had asked to sleep with his wife. "Bathrooms? There are your bathrooms," he pointed at two wooden contraptions. The makeshift toilets were in actuality a big metal oil barrel cut in half. Wooden planks with holes cut in the center were then placed over the barrel halves. The Army called it a field latrine.

I shook my head in disgust. "I ain't taking a dump in that."

Allen shrugged. "Well, what are you going to do?"

"I just won't take dump as long as I'm here."

"We're going to be here for at a least a year," Sarge explained.

I was adamant. "Then I'm not taking a dump for a whole year."

It was a bold statement, especially since MREs and T-Rations were on the menu. And I don't care if you have a cast-iron stomach—the combination of MREs and T-Rats will rust it. You are better off taking an Ex-Lax.

I lasted nearly five whole days without taking a dump. My intestines were bubbling like hot grits. One early morning, I couldn't take it any longer. I woke up in a panic and raced to the field latrine. It had been enlarged. It was now a deluxe model with four toilets. It was also empty. But the stench was foul.

*Cool, no one is inside*, I thought. I could do my business and get out quick.

Soon as I had gotten comfortable, the battalion chaplain walked in, sat down right beside me, and opened up the good book.

By the sound of it, the chaplain hadn't taken a dump in two weeks! Between the two of us, it sounded like the Guns of Navarone. I don't know if you have ever wiped your butt right in front of someone, but it is a very humbling experience. You're thinking, *How many times do I wipe? Did I wipe enough? Do I look at it?* It's a lot of pressure. It was tough—but two weeks later, I might as well have been a Neanderthal. I could take a dump at halftime on the fifty-yard line during the Super Bowl and not be embarrassed.

**W**AR IS HELL. BUT IT IS ALSO VERY BORING. AFTER WE pitched our tents and unpacked our gear, we sat around and waited, and waited, then hurried up and waited some more.

"Biological weapons, my ass," KD cracked. "We gon' die from boredom."

We did train a little bit, and of course had the requisite guard duty, but the majority of my day was spent playing the black soldier's favorite card game, spades. I might have been barely proficient at my job, but I became a world-class spades player.

"Big Joker!" I'd taunt the opposition, flinging the card down with a flick of the wrist until it made that perfect "pop!" on the makeshift card table. KD and I rarely lost, even though we rarely cheated.

I also spent a lot of time listening to my Sony Walkman. One of my bags was lost in transit, so I was left with just three tapes by three acts: Guy, Pebbles, and Sherrick, an R&B half-a-hit wonder. Not really the top three albums I'd have picked to have with me on a desert island, but since I was in a desert I had to make do.

"Baby…don't leave me…I'll love you always," I sang along with Pebbles. I listened to those tapes so often that I can still sing the lyrics of every song that was on them.

Listening to all those love songs about women was hard to stomach since there were no women to love. I was assigned to a combat unit, which meant no women allowed. As it turned out, I did not encounter a woman in the flesh for eight months.

One thing that broke the monotony was the constant threat of a chemical attack. It was constantly drilled in our heads that such an attack could happen at any moment. Our NBC [nuclear, biological, and chemical] gear consisted of a mask, pants, jacket, gloves, and boots. Fully suited and booted, it was nearly 100 degrees inside the whole get-up. According to the Army manual, a soldier under chemical attack has just nine seconds to don the mask.

Add to that the life-and-death pressure of the situation, and it might as well have been one second. The first time we had a real threat, there was widespread panic in our tent. The call came in a little after one a.m.

"Gas! Gas! Gas!" screamed the night guard as he ran through the tent, slapping our feet to wake us up. The guard yelled that platoons of Iraqi tanks were headed our way. That meant we were dead meat, because all we had were a few Hummers equipped with machine guns. Sleepy-eyed soldiers were jumping up and bumping into each other. Ten seconds had passed and only one person had on his mask—and his was on backwards.

I frantically searched underneath my cot. "Dammit, where is my mask?" I yelled.

A soldier next to me had given up and sat on his cot crying. "My wife? My kids? I don't want to die."

Just as suddenly as it started, the threat was over. Another guard ran into our tent with the news.

"All clear! All clear! All clear!" he yelled through his own gas mask. His muffled voice sounded like Darth Vader with a cold. We learned that a nervous operator somewhere thought he heard or saw something, overreacted, and sent out the alarm. The fake alert spread like a chain letter. It would be the first of many.

"Ha!" KD joked, pointing at guys around the room. "Y'all was scared."

The soldier who was crying next to me turned over on his cot, covering his face. Others laughed it off.

"Hell yeah, I was scared." I didn't have any tough guy illusions.

Moments later we fell back to sleep, albeit a little lighter this time. One thing was certain: if the attack had been real, we all would have died.

It took less than two weeks to see my first action. When it came, it was sudden and painful.

"Medic! Medic!" I yelled. The pain and blood spurting was unbelievable. "Oww, my hand!" I jumped out of my FIST-V limping and holding my wounded hand. I was growing faint. "Medic! Medic!"

My chief, Sergeant First Class Allen, heard my cries and wasted no time running to my rescue. He unslung his M16 from his shoulder and knelt beside me. "What happened, Harmon?"

I sheepishly looked at the ground. "I, uh, cut my finger trying to open a can of Chef Boyardee."

Allen was shocked. "You what?"

"Look at it," I moaned, showing him my bleeding finger. It looked like a pit bull had chewed on it.

Ignoring me, Allen went to the vehicle and returned with a cup of water.

He held up the cup. "Stick your finger in there."

I dipped my sliced finger to the bottom of the cup and every nerve in my body exploded. "Ahh!" I screamed, jerking my finger away. "That ain't water."

He grabbed my finger and shoved it back in the cup. "I know. It's alcohol."

It might have been a notch above a serious paper cut, but whatever. I had officially shed blood for my country. I'm still waiting on my Purple Heart.

If there were any person other than Rambo that you'd want to go to war with, it would be a soldier like Allen. He was a dead ringer for the actor Robert Conrad from the 1960s TV series *The Wild Wild West*. Allen was from Morehead, Kentucky.

"Do they really give more head in Kentucky?" I'd often tease.

Allen had no deficiencies as a soldier or military leader. But in the people skills department, he had about as much sensitivity as an old hooker. Although I was a Specialist E-4, he outranked me by three stripes (which is a lot).

I began to notice a distinct trend in my personality. More and more, I seemed to have a problem with authority, odd given the fact that I was a soldier. I fought with Allen daily, mostly about busy work. Sarge didn't believe in idle hands, and he always had something for us to do. Our team consisted of myself, Sanchez, and Johnson, two fresh-faced buck privates. They knew even less than I did. Sarge kept us on our toes. It was always "Harmon, double-check the antenna," or "Harmon, troubleshoot the radio." I'd burn with frustration because each of those tasks involved scores of small parts that were easily lost. I wasted valuable time that could have been better spent polishing my spades skills.

"Harmon," Sarge snarled, catching me once at a card game. "I need you to come break down the vehicle's transmission."

I frowned. "Break what? I'm breaking now. I'm taking a break. Do I look like Mr. Goodwrench?"

My buddies giggled.

"You heard, Harmon? Move your ass right now!"

"C'mon, Sarge, can't you see I'm playing cards?"

Then he got all slave master on me. "I'm the boss. You work for me. So let's go."

I threw my cards down on the table and looked at my lounging, shirtless buddies. "Sorry boys, I'se gwine to go down in da fields." Then I'd stare glaciers at the Sarge.

I hated him just as much, if not more, than I hated Sergeant Wayne—but the difference was that I also respected Allen. The man knew his business and I felt safe following his orders. He knew everything about our job, and that was important because I didn't know jack. But I knew there would come a day when we'd bump heads for real. I was getting sick of his attitude. Here we were, two months in the desert, it was 120 degrees in the shade, and the only thing we were killing was time. However, the good Sarge acted as if we were battling for the Bulge.

One afternoon I was in the driver's seat backing up the FIST-V, which is somewhat akin to driving a double-decker bus. Sarge was on top of the vehicle fiddling with an antenna when I made a sharp turn. I didn't see him but he nearly swerved off—which would have meant a fall of nearly fifteen feet.

"Goddamn you, Harmon," he yelled through the headset. "You almost killed me."

I took off the headset and apologized for not seeing him, but Sarge wasn't trying to hear it. He addressed Sanchez and Johnson.

"You see, Harmon doesn't give a shit about anyone but himself. He doesn't take anything serious. I hope you guys don't turn out like him."

"Fuck you, Sarge," I exploded. I didn't know what came over me. "You don't know a damn thing about me."

Our relationship went downhill from there. I was hoping that we never got into a firefight, because I knew the first person I was going to shoot, and it wasn't going to be an Iraqi.

A S A COMBAT SOLDIER, YOU ARE TAUGHT TO "LEAVE IT ALL ON THE battlefield." It was a phrase our leaders constantly drilled into our heads, and my unit learned early in the war that a soldier could leave a lot of himself on the battlefield...literally.

One lazy afternoon we got the call to muster. The colonel wanted the whole battalion in formation, ASAP.

"What's the deal?" we asked each other as we formed ranks.

No one had any answers, but soon rumors began floating. The black body bag in the back of the colonel's HumVee confirmed those rumors. Inside it was the body of a young soldier, a truck driver just nineteen years old. He had been blown to bits while souvenir hunting. Murmurs reverberated through the formation. This soldier was a likeable guy, well known in the unit. His death was senseless.

"I want you men to see this," the colonel said, his voice filled with iron. "Because this is what happens when you lose your focus."

He unzipped the bag. We winced. The mix of blood, bone, and gore was sickening. Both of the soldier's arms and legs were blown off. The colonel explained that the driver had gone exploring through an area recently bombed. He picked up what he thought was a souvenir, but it turned out to be an unexploded bomb. For the sake of a memento, his family was left with only memories.

"Don't let this be you," the colonel warned. "Bombs don't kill soldiers, stupid soldiers do."

I promised myself to never go hunting for war trinkets. Neither my buddies nor I believed an Iraqi bayonet or uniform was worth our lives. None of us wanted to wind up in a wheelchair rolling down the street in a VFW parade.

KD pulled me aside. "Promise that if I step on a landmine or lose an arm, you'll just shoot me?"

I gave him a firm handshake. "Only if you promise to do the same for me."

Our mortality became a daily topic of discussion due to the stepped-up air campaign. The smell of war was in the wind. The horizon seemed to be ablaze with constant explosions courtesy of the United States military. Each night on guard duty, we witnessed the world's largest Fourth of July fireworks display. Tomahawk missiles launched from battleships in the Persian Gulf streaked through the sky like giant bottle rockets. Twenty-five thousand pound "dumb" bombs made the ground rumble beneath our feet, even when they landed miles away. I could only imagine what they did to the Iraqis they landed on.

*God, get me out of this place*, I prayed.

The prospect of death was everywhere. Landmines littered the ground. At any second, a stray artillery shell could rain down from the sky. And the threat of poisoned air was constant. Dealing with combat conditions can be a double-edged sword. Memories are what keep you going, but memories can stop you dead in your tracks. I tried not to think of home, but it was too hard not to think of my mother's love or her home cooking. There was no way for me not to hear Pop's advice or humorous insults in my head. Would I ever again smell a woman's sweet perfume? Or feel her gentle touch? Would I ever again drive a car, or simply watch a movie? My life at that moment was one huge question mark. I lived from day to day and thought to thought.

But in combat, thinking too much can get you killed. It was no longer safe inside my head. With the ground war about to begin, the only safe place now was with God.

When we got the call to mount up, I had the honor of driving into battle. From my seat, I had a 180-degree field of vision. What I saw awed me. Huge plumes of smoke blanketed the battlefield. The sight of it sent a shiver up my spine.

The fog of war.

To my right and left as far as my eye could see were the most technologically advanced machines in our military arsenal. Rumbling along at thirty miles an hour were Bradley infantry fighting vehicles armed with 25mm "Bushmaster" chain guns and TOW anti-tank missiles. Those things could slice an Escalade in half like a stick of warm butter. Next to them were scores of seventy-ton M1 Abrams battle tanks. Buzzing overhead like giant steel dragonflies were Black Hawk and Apache helicopters. Even higher in the sky were the supersonic birds of prey: F15 Eagles, EF111 Ravens, and F16 Fighting Falcons.

I had never been the most patriotic of soldiers. By the time I got to Iraq, I hated the Army so much that I sometimes crossed the fingers of my left hand while saluting during the National Anthem. But being smack dab in the middle of all this military might gave me an adrenaline high worthy of a Viking berserker.

"Whoooo! We're coming to kick your ass, Saddam!" I roared, knuckles white from gripping the steering levers.

Circling in the distance like massive vultures were B-52 bombers, their deadly payloads carving meteor-sized craters in the sand. The battlefield was blanketed in acrid smoke. Combine that with the spectacular explosions from thousands of 155mm howitzer artillery rounds, and what I was seeing was a page ripped right out of the Book of Revelation. Apocalypse.

*There is no way they can beat us*, I thought.

The Iraqis agreed with me, because by the end of the day my unit had nearly two thousand POWs. They were surrendering by the hundreds. We had so many prisoners, we stopped accepting them, instead letting them shuffle behind us as we forged ahead. They were everywhere. It was like driving through a sea of zombies. What struck me immediately was how raggedy they appeared. Their AK-47 rifles were caked with sand or rusted. Most of them wore threadbare civilian clothes and went barefoot.

"What a pathetic mob," Allen observed.

I shook my head pitifully. "They couldn't beat a troop of Cub Scouts."

The gaunt and dirty Iraqis were starving and begged us for food and water. We weren't about to give them our good stuff. From atop of our vehicles, we threw Chicken a la King MREs into the motley crowd and they fought over them like Mardi Gras beads. Days later, we drove straight into a graveyard of gridlock. Our convoy slowed down as drivers rubbernecked at the carnage—miles of burning cars and trucks. I didn't know it at the time, but I was driving near what became known as the Highway of Death, the road between Kuwait and Basra on which the retreating Iraqi army was attacked by our aircraft. The devastation was absolute. Incinerated bodies were slumped over steering wheels or hanging out of windows, burned dry while trying to escape. Dogs gnawed on dismembered arms and legs that littered the road.

I didn't sleep for close to two days. I had called down fire missions that destroyed men and machine alike. Yet I was alive amid so much death. It didn't bother me much at the time, and as we passed beyond the destruction, it still didn't bother me. When I finally slept, I slept easy. There would be no post-traumatic stress disorder for me.

Then, before we knew it, the war was over. A loud cease-fire message blasted through our radio, and our long column of vehicles halted to await further orders. Minutes later, the battlefield fell silent. It was like the brief moment after a movie ends, right before the credits begin.

"It can't be over?" Allen asked of one in particular.

It was, and President George Bush told us so himself. It was his voice that came over the radios. A roar of shrieks and laughter exploded from the hundreds of vehicles in our convoy, mine included.

Soldiers jumped from trucks, hugged, high-fived, and danced in the sand. The only soldier who wasn't happy was Allen. He remained in the vehicle, pissed off.

"No…no," He mumbled and banged his fist on his knee. "We've got to go to Baghdad and get Saddam."

I put my arm around his shoulder. "Sorry, Sarge. Maybe next time."

LIKE SEX, WAR HAS TO BE EXPERIENCED IN THE FLESH IN ORDER TO fully appreciate the feeling. And like sex, that feeling can be premature or fleeting, leaving one feeling a bit cheated.

"Is that it?" I asked KD as we lounged in our hot tent.

He was nonplussed as he leaned back on his cot. "What do you want, a ticker tape parade?"

What I wanted was some rationalization of why we were there. Why had I risked my life? Was it all because of oil?

"Harmon, soldiers don't get paid to think, we get paid to do," KD explained.

I knew the phrase well. We were just pawns on a global chessboard.

Well, I vowed never again be a pawn. I wanted to be a king. But now that I had my life back, what would I do with it? Most of my buddies who were being discharged were planning to become police officers or firefighters.

I had been so sure that I was going to die in the desert that I'd given scant thought about the future. What do I do now? I wondered on the plane ride back home.

I didn't want to end up working at one of the chemical plants back home in Lake Charles. I'd seen the blueprint growing up. A wife, 2.5 kids, a little ranch-style house with a truck and car. I didn't want to bust my ass for twenty years at one of the plants only to find out from an oncologist that I had cancer from inhaling polyethylene or some other poison. There I'd be, lying in the hospice, thinking, Damn…I fell for it again.

No, I didn't want to be a pawn. I wanted to be a king.

Maybe I needed another year or two to get it together. I actually contemplated staying in the Army a while longer. That thought evaporated minutes after we stepped off the plane in Kansas. The tarmac was quiet and empty except for the yellow school buses that were going to take us back to Ft. Riley.

When the doors of the bus squeaked open I stood frozen in place. I stared at the driver, mouth agape.

"First Sergeant Hall?"

"Get your ass on the bus, Harmon," he ordered.

I sat behind the former Top Hall, and on the way back to Ft. Riley, he told me of how the Army wouldn't let him go with us to Desert Storm.

"They said I was too crazy," he explained. Apparently he did some extra-nasty stuff in 'Nam, and the Army brass thought Top Hall would have flashbacks or something if sent to Iraq, so they forced him to retire. Left without a job and very little money, he was then forced to drive a school bus for a living. The year before, he'd been commanding 500 combat soldiers. Now he drove a bus route for special education kids. He was bitter and more than a little embarrassed. He acted as if he didn't hear the whispered teasing from a few of his former soldiers sitting in the back of the bus.

"Hey Top, what you do on the weekend, deliver pizza?"

"Twenty-eight years, I gave em'," Top Hall said, ignoring the taunts. "And they put me out on my ass."

I shook my head. That was just like the Army, I thought. When you first go in they give you a gun; when you leave, they give you the boot.

When we arrived at Ft. Riley, the streets were clogged with people holding signs that read "Welcome Back" or "Heroes." There were thousands of people. Some were holding sparklers, and fireworks were going off in the sky. Women were screaming.

"There's your parade," KD smiled.

Women we didn't even know were walking up and kissing us. Confetti fell all around us like in Times Square at the end of World War II. The noise of the cheering and laughter was overwhelming. It was hard not to get caught up in the revelry. I didn't feel like a pawn anymore.

I'm going to be a king, I thought, hugging the slim waist of a cute and curvaceous stranger. By the morning, I'd know her well.

The next few days were a blur as I prepared for life after the Army. I still didn't know what I was going to do with the rest of my life, but God had given me a second chance and I would make the most of it. God had put me through the fire for a reason. I was only twenty-one years old, and I felt like I had seen more than men twice my age. I had traveled the world. I'd gone to war, tasted combat, and emerged unscathed. I didn't know what the future held, but one thing was certain. Guinn Street wouldn't be the end of the road for me. God spared my life, and for that I would be eternally grateful.

While in the desert, I'd begun to get in touch with my spirituality. The threat of losing life and limb has a way of bringing you closer to the Almighty.

*God, if you just...* was a phrase I often uttered. I never was a regular churchgoer, but I vowed that if I made it back in one piece I would go to church the first Sunday I could. We returned late on a Thursday. I still planned to attend church services on Sunday. However, for the next two days I planned on raising hell. I knew my soul was in jeopardy when I checked my bank account.

It hadn't registered that while I'd been away, I had been depositing each check and not withdrawing any money. I went to war with five bucks in my pocket and came back with the same five bucks—there had been nothing to spend it on. Now, my bank account held $15,000.

After the ATM denied my initial request for $15,000, I settled for $200. That would be more than enough for a three-piece white-meat chicken meal with an extra biscuit at KFC and a 40-ounce bottle of Old English 800. Oh yeah, plus a bag of weed, some condoms, and gas money to get to Joanne's house in Topeka. The next two days were an orgy of malt liquor, chicken wings, thighs, and, um, breasts....

My last two weeks in the Army were bittersweet. I was excited to once again become a civilian, but I was sad to be leaving behind my good friends. KD and Drew were like brothers. The going-away party for me was like a surprise birthday party at a funeral home. I even wore black. Drew got drunk, threw up, and cried. KD went outside to a car with a girl for half an hour and came back with a Cheshire cat grin on his face and his shirt on backwards. At the end of the night, drunk and choked up with tears, we all hugged and promised to get together later in life. The next afternoon, I was back on Guinn Street. And just like that, the Army became a part of my past.

I KNEW THAT I HAD BECOME A MAN WHEN, ON MY FIRST DAY BACK, Pops took me to Bear's, his favorite underground haunt. From the outside it looked like a regular house; inside, it looked like a house of ill repute. Pops was like the Pope in there. Everybody knew his name, shook his hand, or slapped him on the back. He reveled in the attention. Although I was twenty-one, I still didn't feel old enough to be in there. The hard stares from the grizzled patrons guzzling Old Kentucky at the bar made me feel as if I needed to be armed. The median age in Bear's had to be fifty. Plus, the old men there looked liked they carried weapons…but not guns. Old men like them were from the old school. They carried knives.

"I'd rather get shot than stabbed," Pops used to tell me. He would know, since he'd been both shot at and stabbed. Like many Vietnam vets, there was a whole part of my father's past that he never talked about, but the battle scars were written on his body.

Pops led me to an empty table in the back and ordered a round of Miller Lights.

"Whoo!" I sighed, sipping the cold beer. "For a moment I thought you were going to order a Schlitz."

Pops smiled. "You don't have enough hair on your chest for Schlitz."

I leaned back and laughed. "I don't have enough hair on my balls for Schlitz."

Pops wasted no time and got right to the point. "So why in the hell do you want to move to Atlanta?"

I knew it was coming. Ever since I had told him that I wanted to move to Atlanta, he'd been on my case.

"Pops, I feel like it's the place for me. I need a new start. I prayed about it, and God told me this is what I should do."

Pop's expression made it clear he was against God's plan. "You should stay here and go to school.

"What?" I frowned. "I can't stay here."

The only school in Lake Charles was McNeese State, a small and predominantly white public university. There was no way I was going there. If I did, next thing I'd know, I'd get one of the locals pregnant, and then have to apply for a job at the chemical plant or Cox Cable.

That wasn't the only reason I wanted to move. There was also the matter of a beautiful woman I'd met in Atlanta the last time I was on leave. But my father could always read me like a cheap novel.

"Byron, that money is burning a hole in your pocket. I know you're itching to blow it," Pops cautioned. "You should save some of it. Don't blow it on some bimbo."

Here it comes, I thought. *Son, why don't you loan your old dad a taste?*

Pops cleared his throat. "Why don't you let me hold a taste?"

No dice. I was now old enough to blow my money on whores. That was a lesson I definitely planned on learning the hard way.

I stiffened in the chair and looked my father right in the eye. "Pops, I'm outta here."

He met my gaze and raised his bottle in the air. "A hard head makes a soft ass."

I gave him a confused look. "Huh?"

"But you're a grown-ass man," he continued. "I wish you luck."

I clanked my bottle against his. "Thanks, Pops."

He took a healthy swig of the cold beer and smiled. "But I know your ass is going to be back here, broke."

Armed with that vote of confidence, I began packing for Atlanta. Before I left, I was eager to spend some time with my buddies from the neighborhood. I was hoping to pick up where we left off four years earlier. But by my second day back it was apparent that time was going to treat some of us differently.

I walked down the street pausing at every other house to say hello to a neighbor. I was like a politician on the stump. It seemed that only my buddies' parents were home. They all greeted me excitedly, but they all had a strange expression on their faces. I could tell they were happy to see me

home in one piece, but something was off. I couldn't quite put my finger
on it. The first house I visited was Miny Mo's, but I was told that he had
skipped town to join the Peace Corps and had vowed never to return.

*He always said he was getting the hell out of Dodge*, I thought.

I then knocked on Little Harold's door, but a stranger answered. She
explained that Harold's family had moved away and now his cousins lived
in the house. The young lady then dropped a bomb on me. Harold was in
jail for gangbanging and dealing drugs.

"In jail?" I said, shocked. Not Handsome Harold? He sang in the
church and had a monopoly on all the short girls in town. "What about
his brother?"

His cousin sighed and told me that he had died from AIDS.

I nearly grabbed my heart. I exhaled deeply and kept on walking, but
I was scared at what else I'd find. This was reminiscent of the tragic time
I came home from Germany. A few doors down I passed LaRon's house.
I stopped dead in my tracks. My jaw, along with my heart, sank to the
pavement.

"LaRon?" I asked, slowly walking up the driveway. I couldn't believe
my eyes. He was half asleep in a wheelchair. A wheelchair? My buddy was
pale and sickly.

LaRon blinked awake and smiled weakly. "BH?"

I shook his hand. His grip was limp, his skin clammy.

Speechless, I just stared at him. Pound for pound, LaRon had been
the toughest guy in the neighborhood. He was the king of stunts. For
Chrisssakes—he was the black Evel Knievel! He should be sitting on a
motorcycle, not in a wheelchair.

"I got kidney problems, B.," LaRon said, his voice barely above a
whisper. He looked down at his gaunt body. "I need a transplant."

He also had epilepsy and a bad heart. It didn't seem fair. We were just
twenty-one. Our whole lives should still have been ahead of us, but for
LaRon, life was now a daily struggle. I was nervous for him. A few years
earlier, Kevin Hardy, the neighborhood comedian, had died after a long
bout with kidney disease. Dazed, I nearly turned back home but instead
walked up the block to Nelson and Craig Joseph's house. The backyard
court was empty. It seemed odd there wasn't a pickup basketball game in
progress. The Joseph brothers were gone, I learned. They had moved to
Dallas.

*Dallas?* I was confused. *What are they doing in Dallas?*

Nelson was supposed to be playing football at Grambling University. I later found out from friends around town that he had left school. He then turned up at McNeese State, but soon left that team too. I never found out why, but I was definitely disappointed. Nelson was our hero, All-World in everything. He was supposed to go to the pros.

Everywhere else I went, it was the same basic story. Moved away... dead...in jail...on drugs. The few friends I ran into were cold and distant. I got the impression they felt I was superior because I had left home and been around the world. A few were jealous that I didn't need them to go half on a forty-ounce of Old English 800 anymore. It was depressing.

I walked back home and slumped on the couch. If there was any doubt in my mind about leaving, it was all erased that afternoon. There was no way I could stay in Lake Charles now. It was obvious why the older people in the neighborhood had looked at me with that weird expression. They were surprised to see that I wasn't dead, or in jail, or high.

Before long, I was on my way out of Lake Charles to Atlanta in my Chevy Beretta.

Now, I've always paid attention to omens. For instance, I knew it was not a good sign the time I was in bed with a married woman and heard a loud violent banging on the front door, followed by the phrase, "I'ma kill that nigga!"

Or the time I was standing up in bed in a drunken stupor, pissing all over my mattress, when out of nowhere Pops clicked on the light.

These were obviously bad signs, even to an untrained eye. So why did I not think it was a bad omen when halfway to Atlanta, my car caught on fire?

I tried to accelerate, but the harder I pressed the gas, the slower the car became. Then I lost control of the wheel. I zig-zagged all over the interstate trying to gain control. I pulled over just in time to miss an eighteen-wheel semi. Safely on the shoulder, my brand-new Beretta stalled. I jumped out and ran down I-10, fully expecting the car to explode at any moment. I waited and waited, but no explosion. When the smoke cleared, I checked around the car for damage. Although I knew as much about engines as I did about Einstein's theory of relativity, the car seemed to be okay to me. I turned the key in the ignition. Nothing. Just an odd clicking sound. I got out of the car and stood pathetically beside it, hoping for a Good Samaritan to stop.

I sat back in the car and slumped over the steering wheel. I stared at the sky with an apple-sized lump in my throat. It would be dark soon, and I was a black man stuck on the side of the road in Alabama with $1,500 in my pocket. I was a hate crime just waiting to happen.

*Lord*, I prayed, on the verge of hyperventilating. *You have never let me down in my life. I am about to lose my damn mind. I need your help and I need it real bad. Lord, if you get me out of this jam I will take this $1,500 in my pocket and buy Christmas presents for poor kids in Atlanta.*

I stuck the key in the ignition again and turned it. The Beretta coughed to life.

"Thank you, Jesus," I said.

I eased the car back onto the interstate. The fastest it would go was twenty miles an hour, but that was good enough to get me to the next exit where there happened to be a garage. A mechanic fixed the ruptured transmission fluid line quickly, and in no time I was back on the road.

*Thank you, God*, I softly prayed while turning the volume up on Pebbles. *I won't forget about my promise to get those Christmas presents for the poor kids of Atlanta.* I patted my pocket and smiled. Hell, it was only June.

# ACT III

## The Dark Age

OVING TO ATLANTA BECAME A WATERSHED EVENT IN MY LIFE.
Aunt Joyce, my mother's sister, was gracious enough to let me
live rent-free in her spacious home in Stone Mountain. She was
divorced, with three children, Katina, Jason, and Mike. Aunt Joyce became
one of my most important influences, and basically helped transform my
philosophy of life. She was smart, successful, and career minded. At the
time I was really confused. I'd been away from regular society for four years
and adjusting was very hard. I was bitter, cynical, and stuck in what my
aunt dubbed my "angry black man" phase.

"But the white man don't want me to be successful," I'd whine.

Aunt Joyce would give me a look that made me feel twelve years old.
"Byron, you better learn how to interact with white people, because nine
out of ten times it's going to be a white person who is going to hold the keys
to your opportunity."

"I'm no sellout," I said defiantly.

She waved me off dismissively. "Boy, I didn't say kiss any ass. You can
maintain your dignity and pride and work the system at the same time."

This was true—because Aunt Joyce was a true master of the system. She
and all the women in her neighborhood were what I'd call *Essence* women,
the type of successful modern black women who are always being profiled
in *Essence* magazine. In hindsight, I believe that God brought me to Atlanta
so that she could tutor me, and in particular, teach me humility.

Meanwhile, God was humiliating me. First, the transmission in my
Beretta burned up, causing the car to shake violently at every other red light

and stop sign before loudly conking out. One time, I took a very attractive young lady out on a date, and she jumped out of the passenger side door, thinking my car was possessed. It was beyond embarrassing.

Next, nobody told me that Atlanta was on the outskirts of Sodom and Gomorrah. Temptation was everywhere, and I tried to pick up every fallen angel I met. In two months, I blew nearly $15,000 on clothes, liquor, and lap dances. I was "making it rain" like a pro ballplayer. I never did help out those poor kids, unless their mothers happened to be among the strippers I splurged on. I was soon forced to get a job. I immediately started serving a bid at United Parcel Service, otherwise known as "Us Po' Slaves." Along with crab fishing in the Bering Sea, loading trucks at UPS is one of the hardest jobs known to man. For six hours a day, I grabbed heavy boxes off a nonstop conveyor belt, then loaded them onto eighteen-wheeled trucks. I moved thousands of packages a day with only one fifteen-minute break.

Maybe working at the plant back home wouldn't be all that bad, I thought while struggling beneath the weight of a large box.

I lasted three months before I broke down and quit. A few weeks later I was back in Louisiana, flat broke, embarrassed, and feeling like a failure. Other than my regard for my Aunt Joyce, I still get mad when I think about my time in Atlanta. I understood why General Sherman once set the city on fire. I promised myself that if I ever moved back I would have a much better plan.

"Pops, don't say it," I mumbled into the phone. I dreaded making the call to tell him I was leaving Atlanta.

"How much money you have left?" He probed.

"Pops?" I pleaded.

Silence.

"Okay, I'm broke," I admitted. "You happy? Go ahead and say it."

He pleaded ignorance. "Say what, son?'

I rolled my eyes. Sometimes I wanted to choke him. "Okay, Pops, I'll say it. You told me so."

"I wasn't going to say that I told you so," he said.

My eyebrows arched. "Really, Pops?"

"Really," he said. "But I did tell your black ass so."

Jeez. I moved in with Andre, who had recently returned from Saudi Arabia. He had a little one-bedroom apartment in Baton Rouge, and I crashed on the living room couch. My new and improved plan was to attend Southern University. Why not? I was broke, but I still had the GI Bill and a $30,000 college fund. Right?

Wrong.

"I'm sorry, Mr. Harmon," the young registration clerk apologized while squinting at her computer screen. "But there is no record here of you ever signing up for the GI Bill and the college fund."

"Hold on, there must be a mistake," I gritted through clenched teeth. "Otherwise, that would mean that I just wasted four years of my life being yelled at by assholes and marching miles through mud and freezing my ass off in the snow and risking my life dodging bullets during Desert Storm. Check again."

The clerk nervously looked around for security. I banged on her desk to get her attention.

"I want my damn money."

I didn't get my damn money. Instead, I got escorted out. My only recourse was to seek help from my congressman and file a grievance, which would take up to six months. I could still register for school while I appealed, but there would be no dough for the time being. I shuffled home from the registrar's office in a daze. I felt like the biggest fool in the world.

In the meantime I had to find work. The bills were mounting, and I had a grand total of $34 to my name. The only job I could find was seasonal work at Toys R Us. Six months earlier I *was* GI Joe—now I was selling them. How much lower could a brother sink?

A week after Christmas, I was fired.

Three days later I was overnight stocking and bagging groceries at the Superstore.

I augmented my meager earnings by doing temporary work in a 7UP warehouse loading cases of soft drinks. My paycheck was anorexic. If that wasn't depressing enough, my car got repossessed. I had just come from filling the tank at the gas station, too.

*At least I have a girlfriend with a soft shoulder to cry on.*

Make that a cold shoulder. My girlfriend, Tracy, dumped me, too.

"How can you kick a man when he's down?" I asked.

She pointed at the purple hickey on my neck. The love bite didn't match Tracy's dental records. Of course, my cheating had everything to do with her decision to leave me, but I wasn't really thinking straight at the time.

LTHOUGH I WAS STRUGGLING FINANCIALLY, I WAS STILL EATING IN grand fashion, as in Grands biscuits and eggs. I ate that meal nearly every day. My mouth still gets dry when I think of wolfing down those cake-sized hunks of flour. As I lay on the couch, broke and broken-hearted, I even thought of rejoining the Army.

*Those MREs weren't all that bad*, I thought.

The only bright spot was the beginning of the spring semester. I was excited, finally, to be going back to school. Southern University was a big school as far as historically black colleges went. There were more than 12,000 students registered, and most of them actually went to class. As I saw it, Southern had a relaxed open-admission policy which was akin to "don't ask, don't tell." We had some rough characters enrolled there. Pretty co-eds were everywhere, just like on the sitcom *A Different World*. The girl-to-guy ratio had to be at least eight to one. Now, I had just spent most of the last four years cooped up with nothing but dudes. Being among all that estrogen was refreshing. I had one class in which there were only five guys amid thirty girls.

But often, I was actually too nervous to go to class. I couldn't even talk to these young, nubile girls without feeling awkward. Besides, as a twenty-one-year-old freshman, I felt ancient.

Since I was free of distractions like money or a car to chase girls in—I had little choice but to study. I finished my first year with a 3.8 GPA. Initially, I chose economics as a major, but I'd had no idea serious math was involved. I sucked at math. I could count money, but that was about it. I went to Plan B: print journalism. I figured there couldn't be any math involved in that other than counting dead bodies.

My journalism classes turned out to be interesting, and my instructors were dynamic. However, I still struggled to find my niche on campus. One must have a niche at Southern or risk becoming a "regular" student, the kiss of death. You see, Southern didn't have students as much it had stars in training. Status meant everything. If you were a girl, God forbid you didn't have a cute outfit to wear every day. As I saw it, the main cliques were as follows: jocks, hot chicks, hot guys, Greek organizations, rich kids, out-of-state clubs, whiz kids, and drug dealers. I qualified for none of those, so I joined the *Digest*, the campus newspaper, as a features writer. I had no high-minded notions of investigative exposes, or dreams of winning a Pulitzer Prize. I just wanted to be popular.

In the early nineties, the *Digest* was very Afro-centric and issues-oriented. The paper thrived on politics, and I clashed immediately with my editors.

"Byron," my dreadlocked editor, Leah, yelled across the newsroom. "There is evidence of fraud in the financial aid department. Go check it out."

I rubbed my chin as if deep in thought. "I have a better idea. How about I interview the new Miss Southern?"

Another time I found this assignment in my box: *There is an* E. coli *outbreak in the cafeteria. Go check it out.* Instead, along with Craig Johnson, my partner in crime and a world-class artist, I turned in an illustrated spread called "The Top Ten Hottest People on Campus." The students loved it. The papers flew off the newsstands. It was one of the most popular issues in the paper's history. A hundred years ago, I would have been called a "yellow journalist." I didn't care. It worked.

A year later, when Craig and I became editors of the *Digest*, we turned it into a "must read." My profiles and features turned many students into stars. I was invited to all of the best parties. I knew all of the most popular people in school. My little black book started to get new entries daily.

While school was going well, I was still broke. I had no job, and my unemployment benefits had run out. I even applied for welfare and food stamps, but the paperwork was ridiculous. I sat in a hot, overcrowded welfare office listening to dozens of screaming welfare babies while getting hit on by their welfare mommas. There were a hundred forms to fill out. I just wanted some food stamps, not to close on a house! I walked out and went back home to roll pennies and eat biscuits.

Then it happened. I got my GI Bill money! After eight months of wrangling the red tape, my congressman came through. I rubbed my hands together expectantly. I was eligible for $883.58 every month I was in school, and with the back pay, I received a check for $5,000.

I felt like I had hit the Lotto. But after deducting the money I owed Andre for room and board, I was left with a grand total of $200.

Nevertheless, I would have steady money coming in, and to top it off I landed a cushy job selling ladies' footwear at Shoe Spot. Things were finally looking up again.

Then Pops got cancer.

MY MOTHER USED TO SAY THAT THE ONLY THING THAT COULD SLOW Pops down was a bullet. However, my father had dodged bullets his entire life, whether it was in the napalm-drenched jungles of Vietnam or violent juke joints in the Louisiana backwoods. Now, though, cancer was ravaging his lungs. Pops, a lifelong smoker who had always been thin, seemed to drop more weight daily, and suffered through violent coughing fits. Soon, he was even too weak to drive. I would trek the two hours home to Lake Charles from Baton Rouge on the weekends to drive him to chemotherapy treatments in Houston. It hurt my heart to see my father slowly dying. But Pops never lost his sense of humor.

"Keep your eyes on the road, jackass," he'd snap at me in between naps. It was an hour-and-a-half drive to the cancer clinic and it drove Pops nuts to have to ride shotgun. "If cancer doesn't kill me, your driving will."

I rolled my eyes. "If you don't leave me alone, I'ma make you walk back."

If you've never had the chance to see the inside of a cancer clinic, consider yourself lucky. It's worse than any regular hospital. Death is literally in the air. The halls are crowded with terminally ill people being wheeled either to or from chemo treatments, the faces of their family members plastered with the same look of sorrow.

*They look so pathetic*, I thought. I could have seen the same look in any mirror.

Cancer devastates the whole family. I only saw Pops on the weekend, but my mother and Marshall were on the frontlines daily. My mother deserved a Purple Heart for the way she dealt with my father's cancer. Pops was ornery on a good day, but under the effects of the chemo treatments he was downright demonic.

The physical pain he suffered under was unbearable, but the damage done to his psyche was tragic. My mother even had to get rid of his guns for fear that he'd shoot himself—or her. Mom told me many a day she would storm into the next room, hold a pillow to her face, and just scream. She kept that under wraps for a long time. Andre and I never knew. Although he was weak, Pops would put up a brave front for us when we came to visit.

"I'ma kick cancer in the ass," he'd boast.

I'd smile weakly while trying not to stare at his bony wrists poking through oversized shirtsleeves.

Back in Baton Rouge, I went through the motions. As I suffered, so did my schoolwork. Nothing seemed to matter to me. For the first time I contemplated what I would do if Pops died. My father was the glue that held our entire family together. Not only was he Pops to me—he was Uncle Dave to all my cousins and Cousin Dave to all of his. He was always on call and available to help a family member out of a jam.

*If he dies, God, I want to die, too.*

I really felt that way. I nearly lost my mind watching my father waste away. At night I would lie awake in my old bedroom on Guinn Street, my eyes flooded with tears. For the first time in my life, I questioned my faith. I felt like God had abandoned me. Still, I prayed more than a monk. I did more than pray—I begged.

*Why my father? What can I do? God, this isn't fair. Please spare him. If you help me I promise I will—*

It didn't occur to me that God had heard it all before.

I DID MY BEST TO PUT UP A GOOD FRONT. WHILE JUGGLING THE stress of my father's situation with my schoolwork, I also had the stress of working in the 'hood. I thought that with my discharge from the Army, I would be finished with combat.

Working at Shoe Spot taught me the major difference between black people and "Niggaz." Black people get to the checkout counter and pay for their shoes. "Niggaz" grab a pair of shoes off of the shelf and run out of the store.

*I don't know why they're running,* I'd laugh to myself. *I damn sure ain't chasing them for a pair of K- Swiss.*

Apparently, neither was our fat, worthless security guard.

Shoe Spot had three stores in town and the branch I worked in was located on Plank Road, one of the most infamous stretches of blacktop in Baton Rouge, aka "The Big Raggedy." Preachers and prostitutes both walked the Plank. I saw it all at Shoe Spot, from people putting on a pair of sneakers and then "sneaking" out of the front door, to a mother trying to buy baby shoes with food stamps. Meanwhile, our security guard was too busy in the parking lot selling dime bags to fight crime. Hell, I didn't care. I loved selling shoes, especially since I had the good fortune to be the only male working among seven women. I called them "The Girls." After my first week, I had decided that my future was in ladies' footwear. I was the black Al Bundy.

Since I was the only one in college, The Girls, who were all various degrees of ghetto fabulous, called me "College Dude." The Girls were always sick or late. The Girls teased me because I came to work on time and worked extra hours whenever warranted.

The Girls were also robbing Shoe Spot blind.

Some genius at corporate decided there wasn't a need to check inventory. Smart move. He probably works for the Pentagon now. The no-inventory policy meant that as deliveries of shoes and sportswear came in the back door, half of the new merchandise left out of the side door. It took me about a month to notice that once a week, a special "friend" of one of The Girls would come in and stock up on a shopping cart full of stuff but only pay for a bottle of shoe polish. I pulled one of The Girls aside.

"Keisha, what's up with that?" I asked. She looked at me the way a veteran hooker would look at a virgin.

Two days later, I had my own special "friend" buying shoe polish.

When in Rome...

But I took it to a new level. My co-workers feared that we'd soon be co-defendants. I was so bold that I sold cases of bootleg "Daisy Duke" cut-off shorts on campus.

"Psst," I'd stand in a corner and whisper like a drug dealer in the park. "I got them Daisy Dukes...three for ten."

Six months after I started working at Shoe Spot, the store went out of business. We couldn't even have a clearance sale because we had already cleaned the store out.

Unemployed again. Damn, I had been fired more times than a stolen pistol.

But God works in mysterious ways. A few days later, one of my journalism school instructors heard of my plight and suggested I apply for an entry-level job as an archivist at WBRZ Channel 2, a powerhouse local television station. The teacher knew the general manager and gave me a good recommendation. When I arrived for my interview, decked out in a crisp blue suit with red power tie, I quickly realized that my teacher had given ten other students good recommendations, too. But after I introduced myself to Wannette Easterly, the interviewer, and took my seat at the end of the line, my concern turned to confidence. I just had a feeling that I was going to get the job. Maybe it was faith. Maybe it was the power of prayer. More likely, it was the fact the other applicants were wearing Karl Kani jeans outfits or tracksuits and didn't have any copies of their resumes.

"Byron, tell me about yourself," Wannette asked. She was the executive assistant to Bill Vance, the news director. I liked Wannette immediately. She was nice and her smile was motherly, but I could tell by her tired eyes that she was drained from having to interview such an unprepared group of applicants.

I looked her in the eye. An easy smile creased my lips, and I felt a surge of confidence flow through me unlike anything I had ever felt before. It seemed that everything I had done up to that moment had prepared me to answer this one question. Everything. The hot, stinky, sweaty nights washing pots at Piccadilly. The four grueling and hazardous years spent in the Army. The last two years of suffering through dead-end jobs, self-doubt, and inner turmoil. I was twenty-two, but a *tired* twenty-two. The rest of my life depended on my answer. I took a deep breath.

"Ma'am, there are five things you should know about me. I soak up information like a sponge. I am honest. I am trustworthy. I come to work on time. And if I call in sick, send my mother some flowers, because I'm dead."

Wannette let out a hearty laugh. "Byron, I think that you will fit in here nicely."

I looked around at the tastefully decorated walls of the conference room and smiled. "Funny you should say that, because I was thinking the same thing."

This time, when opportunity knocked, I opened the door and dragged his ass inside. I knew right away that working at WBRZ was the chance of a lifetime. I was a sophomore journalism student who was now actually working in the journalism industry. Very few of my instructors had any real-world experience working in television. Also, WBRZ was state-of-the-art. Baton Rouge may have been in the hundredth-largest television market, but it operated like it was in New York City. John Spain, the station's manager, had outfitted the place with the latest in broadcasting technology. We had the benefit of top-of-the-line live and satellite trucks. There was a helipad behind our building for the traffic helicopter, along with a global downlink center. This meant we could get information and video from nearly anyplace in the world—no small feat in the pre-internet era. The inside of the station was decorated with marble floors imported from Italy. The spotless, futuristic newsroom featured computers with next-generation broadcast software. WBRZ was by far one of the most technologically advanced local news stations in the country.

WBRZ was also whiter than Forsythe, Georgia. It was an extremely corporate place. I can honestly say that I never experienced any overt racism there, but I knew it was monumental that a young black man had a chance to work at the station. Most of the students who worked or interned there came from LSU, not Southern. That meant they were white. The journalism school at LSU was named after Richard Manship—the owner of WBRZ. I was under a lot of pressure. I had to make sure that I didn't screw it up for the next brother. As far as WBRZ was concerned, I was sort of like the Jackie Robinson of the Southern University School of Journalism.

My first job was as an archivist, the next species above gofer. I logged or filed scripts and videotapes. I drove news cars to the scenes of stories and to maintenance appointments. I held umbrellas while reporters did their live shots in the rain. I operated live trucks and downlinked feeds in our satellite center. I made coffee and went on lunch runs. I did plenty of things no one asked me to do—like come in early, stay late, or come in on my weekends. In a few short months, I had learned nearly every job in the building. That way, I felt, I knew too much for them to ever get rid of me. I got along fine with the white people at the station and developed a charming style that served me well. Compared to the Army, this was cake, and I didn't even have to sweat or dodge any bullets.

Once again, I was changing, evolving. I was no longer the cynical, burned-out veteran hellbent on wasting his money and chances. I learned a lesson that would serve me well in the future—if I put all of my faith on the line, God would bless me beyond measure.

My hard work was rewarded.

I was also starting to roll in the dough. WBRZ paid me $14,000 a year. I was also getting those $833 tax-free dollars every month from the Army, not to mention the Pell Grants and student loan money. I was clearing close to $2,500 a month and I was still in college! Andre and I moved on up to a plush two-bedroom townhouse in Fox Hills, a gated community. We now had steak to go with those Grands biscuits and eggs. I also traded in my Nikes for a Mustang.

Then my life got even better. I was one of twelve students in the nation to win a National Association of Black Journalists scholarship for a four-month paid internship at *Fortune* magazine in Manhattan.

*Thank you, Jesus!*

He and His father were really looking out for me and mine, because next came the biggest news of all. Pops had finished his chemotherapy treatments and had gone in for a checkup. The tests came back negative. Pops, it seemed, had beaten lung cancer.

A MONTH LATER, CANCER WANTED A REMATCH. BUT THIS TIME IT WAS bigger, stronger, and more aggressive. It attacked Pops's liver. The prognosis was bleak.

"Don't even come in for treatment," the doctor advised. There was nothing more they could do. The doctor gave Pops one month to live—but judging by the pitiful the shape my father was in, I thought the doctor was off by about three weeks.

Pops spent the days lying in the bed, the soft, down-filled covers pulled up to his neck. His face was gray and sallow, his cheeks hollow, his eyes sunken.

I could only stand and stare. I had the world's largest lump in my throat.

"Son, I look like shit," Pops joked. His voice was scratchy and hoarse, his lips cracked.

I couldn't argue. I sat on the bed's edge and held his cold hand. I had always felt strength in that hand as a child. That night, I felt something else. It was despair and the loss of hope. Pops looked terrible. He had lost what little weight he had gained back. His head was bald. His body? Little more than a skeleton.

"Pops, you're going to beat this," I lied.

His eyes flickered. He limply squeezed my hand and smiled. "Son… I'm ready to die."

All the air immediately left my lungs. I held my daddy's hand and cried like a baby, his baby boy. My daddy was a man. What in the hell was he doing, saying that he's ready to die? I had never heard my father say anything like that in my life. Pops was a warrior. A soldier. A Viking. David Harmon woke up with a sword in his hand. How could Superman be ready to die? Soldiers died on the battlefield, not in bed. But as I sat there wiping tears from my face, I sighed and knew the fight was lost. In my father's eyes, I saw a defeated stranger. Pops was already beginning his journey home.

While Pops dozed in a morphine-induced haze, my mother came in the bedroom.

"The doctors said we should put him in a hospice," she whispered.

Later on, Pops coughed awake and weakly pulled himself up in the bed. I rushed over to assist him and help him lean his thin arm on the pillow. Pops fought for every breath. "I want to die like a man in my own bed...in my own home. Promise me that, son."

A few days later, he got his wish. My younger brother Marshall was holding his arm when Pops touched the hand of God.

God was smiling that beautiful May morning when we sent Pops home; the sun was blazing and temperatures hovered in the '90s. The funeral was held in Oberlin, and judging by the throngs of people packed inside the tiny church, the whole town must have turned out to pay their respects. It was hot inside the small wooden church. Mothers waved little square cardboard fans that had pictures of Dr. Martin Luther King, Jr. on one side and the name of the local funeral home on the other side. In the back of the building church mothers cooked fried chicken and fish for after the service. A choir softly sang in the background. As people searched for seats, distant cousins hugged, seeing each other for the first time in years. It was a classic down-home funeral/family reunion.

After viewing my father's body, a person would walk over to my family and whisper, "I'm so sorry for your loss. David was a good man."

My mother, brothers, and I nodded our appreciation, but for the most part, we sat together, lost in our own numb thoughts. I vowed that I would not cry. Pops wouldn't want his representative to do that. That's how I had begun looking at myself, as Pops reincarnated. I would not show any hint of weakness, because he never did. But it was hard when everyone around me was crying, some uncontrollably.

"Oh God, no. Uncle Dave! Uncle Dave! Come back, Uncle Dave!" a female cousin screamed. She had to be carried away. I wanted to leave with her.

Another of my grief-stricken relatives had to be restrained from jumping on top of the casket. "I want to go with him," she cried.

Every now and then, I would glance around the church and smile. It made me proud to see how popular my father was. He was certainly being sent off in style. Since he was a career Army officer and a veteran, Pops was entitled to be buried with full military honors. Nearby Ft. Polk had sent a burial detail. They draped his casket with an American flag and the soldiers who were sent would serve as pallbearers. And once the funeral procession made it to the cemetery and the casket was lowered into the grave, another group of soldiers would fire off their weapons in a twenty-one-gun salute. It was a soldier's send off. Pops would have been proud.

By the time Reverend Bellard made it to the pulpit, the atmosphere inside the church was charged. The small and slight reverend, a dead ringer for Sammy Davis, Jr., led the church in a short prayer before pausing dramatically.

Reverend Bellard took off his glasses and wiped his forehead with a handkerchief for added effect. "You know something, chuuurrch?" he drawled.

"What, preacher?" an old craggy voice from the back asked.

He pointed at my father's casket. "David Harmon was a man beloved by friends and family."

A rippled of "Amens" and "Uh-huhs" echoed through the church.

Reverend Bellard cleared his throat and continued. "Earlier, one of his sons," he paused momentarily and looked behind him at a deacon. "Um, what's the young man's name again?"

"Byron," the deacon whispered.

"Yeah, Brian," the reverend smiled.

"Byron," the deacon corrected him.

"Y'all know what, I'm getting old. Well, the young man asked me if it was okay for him to say a few words about his daddy. What could I tell him?"

"Yes…Lord," a large woman sporting an extravagant black hat mumbled out loud.

The old preacher nodded. "Byron also asked me if it was okay for him to stand in the pulpit while he spoke those few words about his daddy."

Reverend Bellard motioned for me to come up.

"I said young man, if you gon' speak the Word, ain't no other place for you to stand but in the pulpit."

"Amen," the church erupted and roared their approval.

*Lord, please walk with me*, I prayed as I slowly and respectfully approached the pulpit. All eyes were on me. While I scanned the large crowd, tiny beads of sweat formed on my forehead, but I wasn't the least bit nervous. I was representing for Pops.

I was dressed in an olive green suit. No black for me. I wasn't mourning the death. I was celebrating the life. I wiped my brow. The church was silent as I casually reached inside my suit jacket and pulled out a piece of paper. After spreading it flat on the podium, I cleared my throat.

"When I first heard that my daddy had died, my first thought was a selfish one."

Behind me, one of the deacons moaned, "Well?"

"I won't lie, I was scared. I mean what's gon' happen to me, now that my daddy's gone?" I paused to look over at my mother. I mouthed, "I love you" to her. She smiled.

"God told me to pick up the Bible, and I turned to Psalms 34." I could hear people turning the pages of their own Bibles to the passage.

*"I will bless the Lord at all times, his praise shall continually be in my mouth. My soul shall make her boast in the Lord; the humble shall hear thereof and be glad. O' magnify the Lord with me, and let us exalt his name together. I sought the Lord, and he heard me and delivered me from all my fears."*

"Preach, young man, preach," the crowd yelled.

I smiled. "My fears? God's all I need to ease my fears. It is not for me or for any of us to question why God brought my daddy home. That's God's business. I enjoyed and loved my father while he was here, and I will love him forever. I thank him for teaching me how to be a man. But I will not cry today."

I banged my fist on the pulpit. "Not one teardrop. I will not mourn his death, but I will celebrate his life."

The church was frenzied now. People were shouting, clapping, and stomping their feet.

"That boy sho' can preach," my grandma Jessie Lee shouted. I managed a weak smile.

I noticed Andre walking up beside me. He began softly singing, "My Soul Has Been Anchored" *a capella*. Andre always had a wonderful voice, but that day, it was stronger and more beautiful than ever. I don't how he was able to keep a note. I was so choked up, but still did not cry. However, nearly everyone else in the church did. With Andre providing the background music, I spoke of my father's history and how he became saved before he died. To this day, it is a source of amusement to me to know that my father had raised hell his whole life, but God still gave him the opportunity to get to Heaven before he died.

"Pops?" I concluded, walking down to his casket. I placed my hand on it. It was just him and me. "The sun hasn't been as bright since you've been gone. The sky hasn't seemed as blue. And I know the cool crisp air of winter's wind won't feel as cold without you. How can I put into words what I can't understand? How can mere words even praise the greatest man I've ever known? How can I question the reasons why God called you home? I can't. Rest in peace, Pops."

I N A WAY, POPS'S DEATH WOULD BECOME MY REBIRTH.
His passing forced me to become my own man. Never again could
I just call up Pops and ask him what I should do. Now I had to depend
on myself—my wits, and, most importantly, my faith. My daddy's death
brought me closer to my spiritual father.

The first big decision I had to make was whether to take a leave of
absence from my brand-new job with benefits and jet off to New York for
a four-month internship at *Fortune*. Did I add that there was no guarantee
the internship would lead to a job? I sought counsel, and everyone told me
that I was insane to jeopardize such a great job for an internship. Besides, I
could write my own ticket at WBRZ. Given the fact that my job there had
transformed my life and given me some financial freedom, I couldn't argue
with their reasoning. I prayed about it, and God told me I should do it.
When I approached my boss, John Spain, about it, he agreed.

"Byron," he said. "You are a valued worker and I know this big internship
would make you even more valuable to us. Don't worry—you'll have a job
here when you return."

I shook his hand. "Thank you, John, you won't regret it."

"I better not," he deadpanned.

My first day in New York, I got cursed out by a cashier at Burger King.
As I took my time casually scanning the menu looking for just that right
value meal, she lit in to me.

"Hey, can you make your damn mind up?" she scolded me. "Don't you
see the line? The menu hasn't changed in twenty years."

Scared, I flashed back to Basic Training and snapped to attention. "Number one, ma'am."

She mumbled over her shoulder to a co-worker, "Can you believe this guy?"

In addition to psychotic burger flippers, I had to contend with sardine-packed subway cars and world-class panhandlers. I am convinced that you can't call yourself a certified beggar until you've worked the streets of NYC.

One day, I saw a woman lying on a trash-littered street corner wearing nothing but a black trash bag. She didn't even have any shoes on. The trash bag had a huge slit exposing her nearly nine-month-pregnant belly!

*Is this America, or Calcutta?* I thought.

When I first saw the woman, I looked around frantically waving my arms, like, *Somebody please help her.* People looked at me like I was the one wearing the damn trash bag. I was shocked at how these callous New Yorkers ignored her pleas for money, some nonchalantly stepping over her bare, crusty feet. I reached in my pocket and gave her everything I had. Twenty-six dollars.

A month later, after being panhandled by dozens of other trash-bag ladies, Mother Teresa herself couldn't get a nickel out of me.

I had a blast at *Fortune.* This was a big-time opportunity at the world's premier financial magazine. Everything was first-class. For one thing, even as an intern, I had an office, business cards, and a salary of $500 dollars a week, more than I was making at WBRZ. I also lived rent-free in a dormitory at NYU. I wanted to intern there forever.

There was some stiff competition, too. At the end of the first week, the company sponsored an intern mixer. One by one, we had to stand and tell the room about ourselves. There were at least fifty interns; all but three of them were white.

"Hi, I'm Becky, from Harvard."

"Hello, I'm Chad, from Dartmouth."

"Good evening, I'm Sarah, from Brown."

I cleared my throat. "What's happening, y'all? I'm Byron from Southern."

"Southern where?" I was asked. "Southern Cal? Southern Methodist?"

*Southern kiss my ass,* I thought, rolling my eyes.

The editors at *Fortune* gave us real duties, too. I conducted out-of-the-

**A**LTHOUGH I CAME BACK FROM NEW YORK WITH CHAMPAGNE TASTES, I was still on a beer budget. My mission in life now became getting back to NYC. The quickest and best way for me to do this, I knew, would be in the field of television, not the print world. I had done my research, and broadcast television paid a lot more. And you needed a lot of money to live in New York. But what would I do? I was still just a lowly archivist—albeit one with tremendous upside.

A few months after I returned to WBRZ, the weekend newscast producer quit and left for a better job in New Orleans. She had gotten burned out working that tough weekend shift. It was a rough schedule indeed, 7 am until 11:30 pm, Saturdays and Sundays.

Her departure left a huge vacuum in the producer ranks at WBRZ. The weekend newscasts were a training ground, and none of the other veteran producers were interested in working that shift. Once again, opportunity was in my neighborhood searching for my address. John Spain called me into his office.

"Byron," he said. "I think you'd make a great weekend producer."

I nodded. "Thank you, sir. But what does a producer do?"

The faintest hint of a smile creased John's lips. "They keep me happy."

This meant it had to be a job that I wanted no part of—but I had a feeling if I didn't accept this job, then John would be very unhappy.

"How much does it pay?"

"I'll give you $19,000 a year."

My eyes got big as paper plates. "When do I start?"

Next to an anchor, a line producer is the most crucial employee on a newscast. A producer has myriad duties, and the wrong decision while performing any of them can be catastrophic. A newscast producer organizes the newscast, decides the stories, and writes them, for the most part. Producers also have to be tough leaders. A producer sits in the control room, times the show, and speaks to the anchors through the receivers they wear in their ears. Good producers are like Captain Kirk, and their control room is the starship *Enterprise*.

My first weekend sailing solo, though, I was pretty much the captain of the Titanic. After two weeks of training, I was thrown to the wolves. (I would learn that this was a common producer-training technique.) I came in at 6 am, an hour early, raring to go.

When I walked into the newsroom it was empty. Not a person in sight. I wondered if it had been a holiday that I had forgotten. It wasn't. I would have to walk this road alone.

During the week the newsroom was brimming with activity. There was an assignment desk operated by three people who listened to scanners and fed information to reporters on the street. There were also managers in the newsroom who decided what stories we would cover. And there were plenty of camera people and reporters.

Now, during the weekend, there was only one reporter, one camera person, and myself. I was drowning before I had even put my big toe in the pool. The whole day was a blur of answering phones, stacking the show, writing, and editing videotape. All the while the clock ticked. The show would start at 6:00 pm, not a second early, and not a second late. I was so hungry, and my head felt like Barry Bonds had used it for batting practice. That whole day the only thing I ate was a Snickers bar. I sat in my chair hallucinating about MREs.

Two minutes before the show, I dashed into the control room with the scripts. I was nervous.

I took a deep breath and watched the animated opening to the news begin in the monitor.

"You are watching the WBRZ Weekend News," the announcer read.

His voice was deep and apocalyptic. I soon found out why. It was the end of my world.

The show that I spent all day slaving over went down in flames before my very eyes. The first story in the newscast was about a pedophile priest.

The first line of anchor copy was:

*This man is wanted for an unspeakable crime against a child.*

Nothing is wrong with that copy, right? Oh, nothing except that at the same time we mistakenly rolled video of Charlie Gibson, at the time the anchor of ABC's *Good Morning America*. I had just called a network anchor a pedophile. Can you say "lawsuit"?

"Oh shit no...wrong video," I screamed and waved my arms. Too late—the damage was done. The tapes had been loaded out of order and none of the tapes matched my scripts. It was horrible. Sylvia Weatherspoon, my anchor, was talking about Saddam while we were showing O.J. Simpson, or she was talking about China and the nuclear threat, but we were showing video of Baton Rouge folks at the local rice festival.

I was convinced that I would be fired. Monday, I was called in to John Spain's office. I had cleaned out my desk and brought in my ID badge, fully expecting to get sacked.

"Byron, I wasn't happy this weekend."

I sat slumped in the chair across from him thinking, Neither was I.

"But you are going to make me happy this weekend, right?"

I perked up. Another chance?

"Of course, John. I promise," I said before racing out the door.

"Wait," he called out. "If you screw up, you're gonna have to come and see me again. You don't want to see me after you've made me unhappy twice. Capiche?"

Sitting behind his big mahogany desk in his spacious office, John looked like Tony Soprano. His threats weren't idle either. I have seen him whack people on the spot for being inefficient. The worst transgression one could commit was saying, "I don't know, John." One time he simply pointed at an assignment editor, then pointed to the door. That's how he fired her. John was cold-blooded, but I knew he liked me.

"Don't worry, John," I said. "I don't ever want to see you again."

I studied and prayed with the same intensity as when I had to qualify during BRM week in Basic Training. That next weekend, my show was great. We had no problems.

I quickly grasped the fundamentals of producing and discovered I was becoming very good at it. Soon they let me fill in on the main shows during the week. I gladly skipped classes to fill in. I was still a full-time student, supposedly, but only going part-time. The way I saw it was that here I was, a twenty-two-year-old black male college junior producing at the number-one TV station in the market, and doing it well.

I began paying less and less attention at school. When I did go to class, I argued with my instructors over the correct way things are done in local news.

I also started making a name for myself in the broadcasting industry by going to seminars and participating on panels. These were great for networking. And a young black male producer who can get the job done is one of the hottest commodities in the business. There are very few black males who produce, and every station wants one on their staff. It was at a "Minorities in Management" seminar that I received two sweet offers to jump ship. One was from Katherine Green, an executive producer in Tampa and a woman who would figure prominently in my future. The other, more substantial offer was from Peggy, a news director in Tulsa, the nation's fifty-sixth-largest market. She wanted me to come and produce her weekday 5:00 pm show.

"Whoa!" I said. "How much?"

"Thirty-eight thousand dollars."

"Whoa!" I would be making a nearly fifty-market jump.

The 5:00 pm news show was huge—this is one of the main news shows any local station produces—but I would have to quit school to take it. What would I do? Again, I consulted with a few folks and they told me I was crazy to quit school. As I always did when faced with a big decision, I went back to my trusty ritual: I would pray all night, and whatever God put on my heart was what I'd do. Well, God advised me to go. So I left.

I KNEW TULSA WAS GOING TO BE AN ADVENTURE WHEN, ON MY first day at work, I found out that shoes were optional. My boss, Peggy Phillips, set the example.

"Welcome, Byron, we're so glad to have you on board," she smiled, motioning for me to have a seat in her office. Her smile was infectious, but when I looked at her feet, I did a Scooby Doo–style double-take. She doesn't have any shoes on!

I thought maybe Peggy was just being comfortable in her office until she gave me a tour of the newsroom, barefoot. She then conducted an afternoon news meeting, barefoot. Then at the end of the day, she walked out into the parking lot, got into her car, and drove home, barefoot.

*What is this,* The Beverly Hillbillies? I thought.

But Peggy, a free spirit, was one of the brightest and best bosses I would ever have in the business. She created a comfortable work environment free from gossip, where a person was treated with respect, and free thought was encouraged.

And that's what got her fired.

The local news business is a shark pool, and there was blood in the water at Tulsa's KJRH Channel 2. The station, a perennial also-ran in the ratings, was in the midst of a restructuring. Peggy had been brought in to shake things up. She had hired a bunch of new people and was in the process of overhauling the whole on-air product. She had some great ideas and the station was starting to see some improvement, but not enough in the eyes of upper management. While Peggy was turning around the station, she should have "turned around" herself—maybe then she would have seen the knife coming toward her back. (More on that in a moment.)

Meanwhile, I really struggled as a producer my first few weeks. This would become a reoccurring theme in my career. The first few weeks were always the hardest. I was alone in an unfamiliar city, without any friends or support system. At work, I had to learn a new way of doing things, a new computer system, and most of all, new people and personalities. I screwed up scripts, was slow making decisions in the control room, and no one reached out to help me. It was survival of the fittest.

Did I mention I was the only black producer there? Later in my career, it became no big deal to be the only black producer, but at the time it left me filled with self-doubt and questions.

Am I good enough?

Do they think I'm here because of affirmative action?

Everyone's motives became suspect. My paranoia made me feel even more alone. I thought most of the white people wanted me to fail, especially one particular director. Dirty blond and blue eyed, he looked like a trailer-park gigolo—or better yet, a poster child for the Hitler Youth.

He pointed out every little mistake that I made. I mean, there was no grace period for me. I was so stressed out that every day after work I would go home, take a Tylenol PM, and go straight to sleep so that I wouldn't have to think about how stupid I was. I woke during the night and counted the hours until I had to be back at work. I had no social life at all, not even on the weekends. I put up a strong front at work, but my nerves were frayed and inside I was a high-speed train wreck. It was no way to live.

And to add insult to injury, my grandmother, Jessie Lee, died from a stroke. Her death crushed me and nearly tore the family apart. She was the glue, the backbone of her family. We've never been the same since. I've visited Oberlin only once since my grandmother's death.

I found solace in my relationship with God. I hit upon a technique for dealing with my problems. I would think about all of the past problems that I had been able to overcome with God's help. They were many, but the memories of the triumphs gave me strength to deal with the hardship. I felt I couldn't go back home to Guinn Street. I had no choice but to persevere.

I started to study my every movement at work. I dissected every decision I made. I came to work early and stayed late. I taped the other producers' shows and made their weaknesses my strengths. I got my hands on every possible study aid from media think tanks like the Poynter Institute and the Radio and Television News Directors Association. No other producer was doing that.

Gradually, I began to rack up consistently great shows. That gave me confidence. I became the go-to producer to handle breaking news and specials. I was given the responsibility of producing high-profile events like a 48-hour live broadcast of the Children's Miracle Network Telethon, and eighteen hours of continuous coverage of the anniversary of the Oklahoma City terrorist bombing. On that particular day I produced five newscasts by myself.

In a few short months, I rose to become the best producer in the shop. The golden-haired director had run out of mistakes to point out.

Meanwhile, I was feeling like an extra on the set of a soap opera. Peggy was in big trouble. The details of what went down are sketchy, but word was that certain factions in the newsroom conspired to get Peggy fired. I would find out later that in local news there are always factions trying to get the news director fired. But at the time, this was virgin territory to me. I was but a piranha just getting my fins wet in a pool of sharks. In Baton Rouge, everything was genteel and gentlemanly, at least on the surface. At KJRH, the air was poisoned with intrigue. Machiavelli would have been proud. I kept my mouth shut and head down and kept on typing. I didn't want to end up like Sonny Corleone. I was making too much money. When the smoke cleared, Peggy was fired, the inexperienced executive producer was now the news director, and I was now the executive producer—little old me. Eight months earlier, I had been slandering Charlie Gibson in Baton Rouge, and now I was in charge of newscasts for a whole station?

And they wondered why the station was in last place.

My success in Oklahoma notwithstanding, I still had my sights set on New York. After nine months of producing in Tulsa, I was still too inexperienced to get a producing job in the top market, but I could get close. At the height of my success at KJRH, I received another phone call from Katherine Green, who was now a news director in Baltimore. Katherine eventually became my Godmother. At the moment, though, she was calling to make me an offer I couldn't refuse.

ALTIMORE, MARYLAND IS SOMETIMES CALLED "CHARM CITY," but as I drove into town in the fall of 1996, I didn't see anything charming about it. What I did see were rows upon rows of run-down row houses pushed back against litter-filled streets. I noticed dejected and defeated black folks shuffling along those streets. I observed dozens of cop cars with their lights flashing at numerous crimes scenes. After I week, I saw why the town was also known by a less flattering sobriquet—"Bodymore, Murderland."

Crime was a constant lead story in the newscasts at WBAL Channel 11, my new place of employment. It was depressing to report on all the murders and drug arrests. By the end of my first week, I was ready to skip town. I produced the 6 pm newscast, and once again, I struggled starting out. I had to learn a new computer system and new people. Baltimore was market #21, and I was learning that the larger the market, the larger the assholes who worked there. Not only did I have the director pointing out my mistakes, but also tape editors and writers, too. Hell, even my production assistants had attitudes.

However, I was learning a lot from my new boss. Katherine Green is one of the two or three smartest people I have ever met in my life. She thinks ten minutes ahead of anyone in the room. Her ideas are off the charts. Also, there is no way to win an argument with her. Her logic is way too strong, and she's a world-class talker. It didn't matter how right you were about something—by the time she was done with you, you'd be babbling like a baby. I know, because I've been there. Katherine would have given Johnnie Cochran a headache.

Fortunately, Katherine liked me. She had been recruiting me since even before I'd dropped out of college. I had quickly gotten over my initial struggles, I quickly began to excel again. After three months, I was picked to attend the prestigious Poynter Institute producer seminar. Poynter, based in Tampa, is a premier media think tank. They only pick a handful of people to attend their seminars, which are taught by some of the top names in the business, and Poynter picks up the tab. It's a wonderful thing to have on your resume, and it's also the best place to network for a new job—especially if you are a producer. Katherine was well aware of this, and she tried to get me to sign a contract before I left.

"Don't worry, Katherine, I'm not going anywhere," I promised. "I've only been here for three months." I told her I'd sign when I got back.

Well, a funny thing happened...

You see, there were plenty of executives there who were in the market for a hotshot young producer. I was a big hit at Poynter. By the end of the weeklong seminar, I had job interviews set up on both coasts. For the next few weeks I flew first class for interviews at stations from Los Angeles to Miami. I was wined and dined, and stayed at hotels where they gave you robes and slippers. Meanwhile, I was dodging Katherine and that contract.

"Uh, I'll sign it tomorrow," I'd lie. "My uh, hand hurts today."

I felt terrible about the way I handled the situation. I still do. Katherine had been so good to me—but I was selfish and young, and only had eyes for the bright lights of New York. I was beyond excited when I got the call I'd been waiting for. The call from New York. Bill Carey, the news director of WCBS, called and asked if I was interested in coming up for an interview.

For decades, WCBS had been the toast of the industry, but by the time of my interview, it was just plain toast. It was well known in the industry as possibly the worst station in the country. In fact, its management had recently fired seven anchors in one day. This happened on October 2, 1996, and newspapers in New York immortalized the event with the legendary front-page headline. "Anchors away!" along with their photos. But I didn't give a damn. It was New York. You think the first pick in the draft gives a shit that they're going to the worst team? I was still in the pros. As I sat there listening to Bill Carey give me his spiel, one thing stood out, my new salary. It would be $100,000.

"Huh?" I asked. "Did you say a hundred grand?"

He nodded. "Give or take a few."

**G**OD GAVE ME SOME BAD ADVICE...
*God gave me some bad advice...*
*God gave me some bad advice...*
The phrase echoed inside my head. It drowned out the roar of the airplane's engines. I gazed through the window down at the legendary skyline of New York City and was overwhelmed by fear. No, make that stark terror. My palms were moist and my heart raced. This was it, the big time. I was twenty-four years old and my dreams were realized. I was in the big leagues, the first-place news market. There was no turning back now.

"Care for a snack, Mr. Harmon?" the flight attendant asked.

I shook my head no. I was too busy snacking on my fingernails and wondering if I had bitten off more than I could chew. It was the winter of 1997, and I only had a little more than two years of experience producing. That was a woefully short amount of time, and no right-minded station manager in New York City would normally take a chance on someone with that amount of experience. I didn't even have a college degree. By comparison, most line or show producers had a minimum of ten or more years on the job.

But there was one other difference between them and me. They sucked. I didn't. When it came to producing, I was a prodigy, a savant, an animal. I was constantly refining my craft and learning new techniques. The old guard was fat, lazy, and resistant to change. I figured that it wouldn't take me long to rise to the top, and once I was there I would have my pick of jobs in the market. Nevertheless, I second-guessed my decision.

*Did God give me some bad advice?*

Deep inside my heart, I knew that was impossible. God had never let me down in my life—not even when I had let God down. But I was still human and still subject to human thoughts and self doubt. I was so scared I think I was the last person to exit the plane.

My first few days at WCBS didn't help boost my confidence, either. Once again, I stumbled out of the blocks early. I was the new 6 pm producer—normally, that's the easiest show to produce, because it's only half an hour long. Add in sports and weather, and it amounts to maybe seven minutes of actual news. But I learned quickly that nothing was normal or easy at WCBS. On my first day, in my first morning news meeting, Bill Carey made the 5 pm producer cry.

"If you're not going to pitch an idea that makes any sense, just shut up," he barked at her. Bill is 6'3" with a deep baritone that would make even hardened felons nervous.

There was absolutely no grace period in the newsroom. When you work in a major-market television station, you must hit the ground running or get run over. I was told that I would be trained for a week so that I could learn the systems and style of the station. Well, my trainer called in sick on my second day. I had to produce the newscast by myself.

"We'll throw you in the deep end of the pool today," joked Matt Ellis, my executive producer.

More like thrown to the wolves. The speed of everything was faster than I had imagined. I had to make split-second decisions all day, not just in the booth during the newscast. There was constant turmoil all day, every day. We'd start a typical day deciding to lead that evening's newscast with four people murdered in a New Jersey neighborhood; by lunch we'd be leading with an overturned tanker with 8,000 pounds of spilled fuel on fire, shutting down a major highway; and by the time we actually went on the air, my lead story would be an airplane crash at a local airport.

I had never had to deal with anything remotely as fast-paced as WCBS. And there wasn't anybody who had any sympathy for me—or anyone else—about anything. It was every man or woman for himself or herself. One never knew where the knife was coming from. And not only did I have to worry about my back, but I was also now dealing with high-priced anchors for the first time.

Anchors are paid astronomical amounts of money to be the faces of the station. Their leverage is supreme. They must be coddled, caressed, cared for. I thought that my new anchor at WCBS hated me. Her name was Dana Tyler, and she was as well paid as she was well known in New York City. She also happened to be one of the best anchors in the market. Dana rode my ass so much I felt like coming to work wearing a saddle. Typos, late scripts, missing words…nothing, it seemed, was ever right. In hindsight, Dana was absolutely right about everything, but at the time I just thought she was evil. I hated her. I really did. I would go home with a splitting headache nightly.

There's an old saying that if you can make it New York, you can make it anywhere. Well, I didn't think that I was going to make it in New York. I couldn't believe this was the same city where I'd interned at *Fortune*. Back then it was so exciting. Now it was depressing. The Big Apple was leaving a bad taste in my mouth. I hated my job, I hated my anchor, and I hated my life. That is, until I picked up my first check. After taxes, I made more in a week than I made in a month in Baton Rouge.

"I love New York!" I sang, while dancing around my apartment.

Three weeks later, I was finding my groove, kicking ass and taking names. I went into full-scale war mode. I taped and critiqued my newscasts. I taped and critiqued my fellow producers' newscasts. Hell, I even taped and critiqued the competition's newscast. I took scripts home and rewrote them. I came early and left late. I took my director and anchors to lunch. I became attuned to the shifting winds of power that wafted through the newsroom. I became grateful for Dana, because she made me a much better producer. Her criticisms were dead-on; I wouldn't have lasted a month if not for her.

After a year at WCBS, I was starting to feel like a first-round draft pick playing on the worst team in the league. Our ratings were horrible. The newscasts were fraught with technical glitches and bad writing. Our newsroom personnel had the morale of POWs. The station went through numerous promotional campaigns, like "More news in less time," during which reporters' stories couldn't last any longer than 45 seconds. This nearly resulted in a mutiny amongst a reporting staff used to two minutes or more. Pablo Guzman, one of the station's best reporters, staged his own protest against the practice. Pablo had a legendary history of dissent—in his younger years he had once appeared on the cover of a local newspaper as a co-founder of the Young Lords, a Puerto Rican civil rights organization. He was a hero in the Latin community. He was also very outspoken.

"Forty-five seconds?" He snapped at Matt Ellis, the executive producer. "That's ridiculous."

Matt shrugged his shoulders and gave him that "I'm just the messenger" look.

Later, during the newscast, Dana tossed to Pablo, who was live on location in the Bronx covering a crime story. Pablo quickly set up his story and tossed to the taped news story, called the "package." The package was only ten seconds long! After the tape ended and Pablo was back on camera, he then voiced his tag line in Spanish. When he tossed back to Dana Tyler on the anchor desk, she looked like a deer caught in headlights.

"Um, thanks, Pablo," she said, barely keeping a straight face.

Off camera, Pablo could be heard saying, "Hey, I saved them thirty five seconds."

Bill Carey saw the report on a monitor in his spacious office and erupted like Mt. Vesuvius. He grabbed the nearest phone and started yelling at Pablo.

While other stations claimed they were "New York to the bone," we were just bad to the bone. I felt like we were the laughing stock of the New York City local news industry.

Luckily for me, I had a "fairy job counselor." Out of the blue, I received a phone call from Paula Madison, the news director of WNBC, New York City's powerhouse station. Years later, I found out that Katherine Green had spoken to her on my behalf. Paula, one of the highest-ranking black news executives in the country, is a legend in our industry. I had read about her in *Essence* and *Black Enterprise*. She asked if I was interested in coming to work for her.

"I'd be honored to work for your organization," I said.

Goodbye, WCBS.

WNBC was a whole different ballgame. For one, it was located in the world-famous Rockefeller Center. There were so many stars there it was like working in outer space. On one floor was the "Nightly News with Tom Brokaw" and "The Today Show." Down the hall was "Saturday Night Live." Across from our studio was "The Conan O'Brien Show." Just going to work was an experience. WNBC was first-class all the way. The newsroom was state of the art and immaculate. Above all, WNBC had Chuck Scarborough and Sue Simmons, the dream team of New York anchors. Also on my show at the time was none other than Al Roker.

God gave me some great advice!

However, producing the 5 pm news on WNBC had its drawbacks. The stress and pressure was more intense than at any other job I'd held to that point. For one, WNBC was a financial powerhouse with incredible ratings, and I didn't want to be responsible for any fall-off in those ratings. The station was also owned by GE, which is famous for always initiating new programs designed to increase productivity. A high level of performance was crucial. I felt like an emergency-room doctor. My one solace was the fact that the ratings on my show were phenomenal. Every one of WNBC's newscasts were rated number-one. I was put on the station's fast-track succession program. Life was great. I could have worked there forever.

So I decided to quit.

I F THERE IS ONE THING THAT I HAVE LEARNED ABOUT MYSELF OVER THE years, it is that I am uncomfortable with the idea of being comfortable. It seems that just when I settle into a groove, it's time to shake things up. While at WNBC, I was at the peak of the local-news business. I was in my prime, like Jordan with Bulls…Magic with the Lakers…Clinton before Lewinsky.

Then, one day, Katherine Green called me up again and offered me a job as an executive producer. She had recently become the news director at WTTG in Washington, DC, a station with a storied history. Problem was, most of those stories were sad. I hadn't spoken to Katherine in two years, not since her comment about God's advice. Needless to say, I was surprised.

"You want me to what?" I asked.

"To be my executive producer," she answered.

I frowned at the phone. "I don't really know, Katherine. I'm doing fine here in New York. I love this place and I'm making great money."

She chuckled. "OK, how much?"

"You know me so well."

I accepted the job sight unseen. That was unusual for me, but when I first drove up to the station, I was pleasantly surprised.

*I can get used to this*, I thought.

WTTG was located on fashionable Wisconsin Avenue near Chevy Chase, Maryland. The area is an enclave for Washington's power elite and is surrounded by expensive stores and restaurants.

It was when I first walked into the newsroom that I felt as if I had made a mistake.

*There is no way I can get used to this,* I thought.

Located in a cavernous decayed wing on the third floor of the FOX Headquarters building, WTTG was a dump. The people in the newsroom barely acknowledged me. The place was about as festive as a mortuary. It didn't help that the person I was hired to replace hadn't quit as expected—to add even more fuel to the fire, we had to share an office. I had to take a different job working the early morning shift for nearly a year until she eventually left. By the end of my first week, I was kicking myself for leaving New York. Well, at least the news in Chocolate City would be less stressful than in the Big Apple. Or so I thought.

Here is a rundown of the major stories I covered while in Washington:

- The Monica Lewinsky scandal
- The Clinton impeachment hearings
- The death of JFK, Jr.
- The Gary Condit intern scandal

And years later, perhaps the biggest story in the history of American broadcast news, the 9/11 terrorist attacks. I was so traumatized by covering that story that it's taken me years just to be able to think about that day.

The Tuesday morning in September began the same way every other morning began, with me deep inside the blanket and rolling over in the bed. As usual I had worked the late shift the night before. I didn't get home until after midnight. As the executive producer of newscasts, I oversaw all of our late-night news coverage. It was a demanding and pressure-filled job that left me mentally as well as physically drained. I needed every minute of sleep that I could get, but Rhadia, my girlfriend of a few months, wouldn't shut up.

"Byron, wake up!" she yelled.

"What is it?" I said groggily from inside the bedroom.

"Quick, come see what's on TV," she yelped.

I forced myself out of the bed, wiped the sleep from eyes, and staggered into the living room. When I walked in and saw the footage of the airplanes crashing into the World Trade Center Towers, I gasped.

"My God! What is this, a movie?" I asked, stunned.

"No," Rhadia said, eyes transfixed to the screen. "Terrorists are attacking New York!"

"I gotta go," I said running into the bedroom.

"Where are you going?" Rhadia asked.

"To work."

I came out of the room dressed in a warm-up suit, grabbed a hat off the wall, and ran out the door.

The Beltway heading into Washington, DC at 9 am is normally a parking lot, but on September 11, 2001, the traffic was bumper-to-bumper heading out of the district. I didn't understand why until I turned on WTOP, the all-news radio station, and heard that a plane had crashed into the Pentagon.

*Oh my God, we're at war*, I thought. I gunned my car faster. A sense of resolve came over me. It was a feeling that I hadn't felt since the first day of the ground war during Desert Storm, on the front lines and preparing to go into combat.

Unlike civilians—a term the news business uses to describe viewers—I didn't have the luxury of getting caught up in the magnitude and emotion of the story. I immediately began thinking about the way we were going to cover it. I knew that by the time I got to the station, we would have the helicopter over the scene at the Pentagon and live reporters headed there. I was certain that we were going to have to stay on the air continuously, maybe even for days.

The 9/11 terrorist attacks made up the biggest story to come along since I'd gone into the news business. Up to that point in my adult life, I had been to war and worked all over the country covering major breaking stories—but none of that prepared me for what I saw when I walked into the television station that morning. I ran right into the control room. It was chaos. What we saw happening on the dozens of monitors in front us made us sick. The towers had fallen in a heap of twisted steel and fire and clouds of dust while the Pentagon was burning.

Live continuing coverage is one of the hardest and most intense things a producer can do. It's emotionally as well as physically draining. I didn't leave the control room booth until midnight, and I kept that schedule for the next two weeks. Once the story had leveled off a few months later, our station was hit with an anthrax scare. There were men in hazmat suits in our station mailroom. I didn't open a letter for nearly six months.

Not long after, we had to deal with the infamous DC sniper. The whole DC, Virginia, and Maryland area was held hostage during the month of October 2002. Every other day, it seemed, someone was getting shot at a gas station. It was so bad that I drove my car until the tank was on fumes before I'd get some gas, and I'd pump it by sitting in the back seat of the car and holding the pump with my arm out of the window. I was shocked when the ringleader turned out to be a Black Muslim.

I won five Emmys for our coverage of those stories and others. Once again I got an offer I couldn't refuse—to come back to New York City and WCBS, this time as executive producer. The station was overhauling its morning show and wanted me to do it. I was flattered they wanted me back. The money was great, but it was a risky move. If the new show failed, I would go down in flames. I would definitely be rolling the dice. Everyone I consulted with told me it was a bad decision and would wreck my career. But once again, I prayed, and God advised me to go. By then, I had been in DC for more than four years and I was ready for a new challenge and change of scenery.

I had also become an author. I was making a name for myself as a writer of romantic comedies. I had self-published my first novel, *All the Women I've Loved*, in the summer of 2004. It was a tough, eye-opening experience. After being rejected by nearly fifty literary agents, I decided to roll the dice and start my own company. I called it David and Sons, after my father. I designed the cover, hired a company to print the books, and made deals with distributors. I also hustled books on the street, out of the trunk of my car, and at parties, eventually selling nearly 3,000 of them. That success led to a deal with Simon & Schuster. They gave me a $25,000 advance on my next novel, *Mistakes Men Make*, which came out a year later. My publisher and agent were in New York and I wanted to turn my books into movies, and I felt that I wouldn't be able to do it in DC. The irony was not lost on me that once again, I had to tell Katherine that I was leaving for New York. This time, however, she gave me her blessing.

I COULDN'T WAIT TO GET BACK UNDER THE BRIGHT NEON LIGHTS OF TIMES Square, but when I got to town, somebody had pulled the plug. That's because my first week back, New York City had a major blackout.

It was a hot, humid afternoon in August 2003 when the lights flickered out. By dusk, it was chaos in the streets as thousands of sweaty New Yorkers clogged sidewalks, cursing, while cabs sat gridlocked at dead traffic lights. No one really knew what was going on other than that the lights were out. My lights were out, too. I had worked the overnight shift and was in bed when there was a panicked knock on my door. It was a doorman.

"Everybody out of the building!" he yelled. "Now! Get out!"

My heart started racing as I flashed back to September 11. I thought we were under attack again. I jumped up and grabbed my wallet and a few valuables before running out of the door. When I got to the elevator, my heart sank.

"No electricity," a neighbor informed me. "Gotta take the stairs."

The stairs? We were on the sixty-fifth floor. The stairwell looked like a circle of hell out of Dante's *Inferno*. People were crying. Elderly folks were stooped against walls wheezing or gasping for breath. Disabled people were groping their way down any way they could. I helped a few people down some flights, but by the time I got to the fortieth floor, I needed help too. I was glad it wasn't a fire, because I would have just burned the hell up. Once I finally made it downstairs, I decided to walk the fifteen blocks to the office and try to get some sleep. I bedded down in a tiny closet near the newsroom. I felt like I was in a pizza oven.

Here I am, back in the number-one news market, and I'm sleeping in a damn closet?

I learned the hard way to be careful what you ask for. The main reason I had been recruited to come back to WCBS was because I had gained a reputation in the industry of being able to handle high-priced anchors—of being, as they say, "good with talent." And it took all of my talents to deal with the "WCBS 2 crew," the nickname of our all-star assemblage of morning anchors. Most newscasts in the market had three anchors. I now had six!

It was a daily high-wire juggling act to keep the anchors happy while simultaneously producing an exciting show—not to mention keeping my bosses satisfied with good ratings. The corporate headquarters of CBS is also located in our building, so my show was always under a microscope. I became the Kofi Annan of morning television. One moment, I would be on the phone explaining to my news director what Dave Price, my comedic weatherman, really meant when he had said, "I know I promised you eight inches yesterday, but I guess you're stuck with six," and the next I'd be rushing Shon Gables, the newscast's beautiful featured anchor, to St. Luke's emergency room after she tripped and smashed her head running into the studio seconds before the show began. Plenty of eyebrows were raised when Shon limped into the waiting room holding her swollen eye. The nurses thought we were a couple and all but accused me of beating her. I had to do some fast talking and show my CBS ID card to avoid a domestic violence arrest.

You never know what to expect with morning news. Anything can happen—and these incidents did:

- One morning, one of my anchors referred to former New York City Mayor Ed Koch (pronounced "Kotch") as "Ed Cock." She also said to the sports anchor, "You're Sicilian? I thought you were Italian."
- One of my reporters, during a live report, turned around and asked a heckler, "What the fuck is your problem?" He was later fired.
- During a live animal segment, an African Gray parrot crapped all over an anchor's suit.
- I had to take a phone call from an irate Bill Cosby—one of the heroes of my childhood and youth—who called in to complain about a story.

Some days there was so much tension on the set that it oozed through the screen. It was like an episode of *The Young and the Restless*. Half the time the anchors wouldn't even speak to each other during the commercial breaks, or they would be in my office after the show slandering each other.

Then one day, in the spring of 2007, we had new management and *poof!* All the anchors were replaced.

The change in management began an exodus of people leaving—few of their own accord. Many from the old regime weren't able to handle the harsh new standards being imposed by the bosses.

"Byron, when are you leaving?" many of the disgruntled asked. There was no question that as executive producer, I was feeling the heat, too.

I'd frown. "Why leave? I love my job."

In truth, I did love my job. I may have hated many of the people I worked with, but I still loved my job. Hell, I was getting good at all the palace intrigue. I had studied with some masters, and I figured that if I could dodge real bullets in Iraq, I could also duck knives thrown at my back in New York.

"These are the times when opportunity presents itself," I confided to a few of my trusted lieutenants.

I told them to keep their heads down and not to engage in newsroom gossip. I went on a PR campaign to impress the bosses, and once they saw the way my hand-picked people performed under pressure, we were solid. In no time at all, the smoke cleared, and my team and I (and a brand-new group of anchors) escaped unharmed—in fact, our position was made much stronger by the new faith upper management had in my abilities as a manager. Once we started to see the ratings rise, they left us alone. I was even offered a big promotion, but I turned it down—the timing wasn't right. I had learned when to say "no" to an opportunity. That impressed them even more.

But alas, all good things come to an end, right? Let me be diplomatic and say that as time passed, I became uneasy with the direction of the station. People were getting unceremoniously fired left and right for reasons that I couldn't understand. One guy was fired the day after he came back from burying his father. As a manager, I was privy to some of the back-room discussions and frankly, they left me disenchanted with local news. Poor me, right? I know what you're thinking. But people can only work in an environment that toxic for so long before it infects their personalities. After four and a half years of waking up every work day at 3 am, I began to hate what I was doing. I disliked half of the people I worked with and for. I was sick of all the backstabbing, whining, and crying. I'm sure they were sick of me, too. My heart wasn't in it anymore. I seriously considered a new profession. I even paid an expensive firm to evaluate my skills to see if they were transferable to another field (they weren't). I felt trapped in golden handcuffs.

But in the midst of darkness there were bright spots. I got a new book deal and published my third novel, *Crabs in a Barrel*, a satire on race relations within the black community. I also signed a movie deal with the comedian\actor\director Robert Townsend to direct an adaptation of *All the Women I've Loved*. Robert even flew down from the set of a movie he was directing in Toronto for a table-read of the script. I had reserved a big rehearsal hall at CBS. It was a great experience to see the director in action. The producers had secured nearly a dozen actors to read the script while Robert and the producers worked out the kinks in the screenplay. He was all over the room, critiquing and encouraging the actors. It was a lesson in the art of screenwriting. Afterwards, we went over the script in my office. Robert was so animated that he backed into the wall and broke one of my paintings. I've kept it as a souvenir, and as the source of a good story. The producers are looking at early 2009 as a release date for the film. My fingers are crossed.

Meanwhile, at WCBS there were rumors of major layoffs in the works. All across the country, television stations were downsizing. For the past few years, the news industry has been undergoing a major overhaul. With the rise of the internet, people have far more outlets to receive the news. The audience for evening newscasts is rapidly eroding. Advertising is down and many stations are in a financial freefall. At WCBS, anchors were being asked to take buyouts or, in some cases, 50 percent pay cuts. Not a pretty place to be. It was so bad I was hoping that I would be offered a buyout. I needed a fresh start, a way out.

Once again, I got a call from Katherine.

She had recently accepted a position as vice president of programming for CNN International, based in Atlanta. It was a huge job where Katherine would have to revamp the programming schedule and create some new shows for the network. The interview process was intense. I was grilled twice by Tony Maddox, the brilliant head of the network, and let me tell you, it was not for the faint of heart. But I knew this was the place for me when his first question was, "What have you done recently to enhance your personal growth?"

Soon after, Katherine offered me a position as senior executive producer for programming. It took about two seconds for me to accept. My colleagues at WCBS thought I was crazy.

"International news?" a coworker asked.

"Cable?"

"You're going to leave New York for Atlanta?"

To me, it was a no-brainer. The day I resigned, my colleagues thought I was psychic—because less than two hours after I gave notice, the station canned nearly twenty people. It was part of an even larger bloodbath—more than 150 people were let go at CBS stations nationwide. Not to sound trite, but once again God came through in the clutch. No one could ever tell me not to trust in God.

Three weeks later I was in Atlanta. I had come full circle, and I made good on my promise that if I ever moved back I would have a better plan. But it was an emotional experience leaving New York. I had specifically chosen the news business as my career in order to live there. I loved New York. But I felt this time that I would never be moving back. I had finally gotten the city out of my system. No more crowded subways, $3,500 a month apartments, and crazy taxi drivers. No more covering house fires and NYPD cop shootings of unarmed black men. No more Al Sharpton press conferences.

In my new position at CNN International I would oversee a large staff of top-flight supervising producers, producers, copyeditors, and writers based in Atlanta, London, and Hong Kong. It was a really big job. I would now be covering stories of global significance, and my new job would involve some serious travel.

"More champagne, Mr. Harmon?" Alistair, the British Airways flight attendant, asked.

I nodded and held up my glass while admiring the plush business-class cabin. I couldn't believe it. I was on the job less than a month and I was on my way to London for two days of meetings! Once there, I had to take questions from a roomful of skeptical Brits who now had a new boss—me.

From London, I flew in style to the United Arab Emirates, with pit stops in Abu Dhabi and Dubai for meetings. I was chauffeured around in a convoy of Cadillac Escalades and toured the skyline of Dubai in a sheik's private helicopter. The last time I was in the Middle East, I was living in a tent—now I was in a five-star hotel.

Not bad for a country boy from Guinn Street, huh?

# Epilogue

I AM OFTEN ASKED TO SPEAK TO CLASSES AT LOCAL HIGH SCHOOLS AND colleges. It always tickles me, since I barely graduated high school and never finished college. Nevertheless, I look forward to these informal discussions, where the audience can range from journalism school students to juvenile delinquents. It's no problem, since I can relate to both with equal ease. I am as open and honest as I can with them about my life and my profession without totally turning them off to the business. It's a tough industry that offers great rewards, but it's not for the faint of heart. You have to be a lion if you want to work in the concrete jungle. One of the questions I am always asked is whether I have any advice for them.

I scan the room and make eye contact with as many as I can, and then I deadpan, "Find a new major."

That usually gets a few chuckles. "But seriously," I smile. "My advice is this: never let anything or anyone stand in the way of your dreams and don't just be the best at what you do, be the only one who can do what you do." Pops used to tell me that when I was a little boy. I didn't understand it until I was a man.

I find it interesting that now people ask me for advice. Many of them snicker when I tell them that I get all of my advice from God, like I'm a crazy fundamentalist or something. Well, the joke's on them.

It was God who stirred the wanderlust for adventure in my heart as a young man. That wanderlust has taken me from Lake Charles to exotic locales all over the world. Who knows what might have happened to me if I'd stayed in Lake Charles? Things didn't work out so well for many of the people I grew up and went to high school with there.

It was God who whispered the words of encouragement that steeled my nerves when I was on verge of cracking up in Basic Training. I realized that with prayer, nothing is impossible.

It was God who cloaked me in a veil of protection while men died around me in the desert. With God as your shield, nothing that man can do can harm you.

It was God who comforted me when Pops died, and then, not so long after, my grandma Jessie. In death there is also life.

I've come a long way since those hot summer days on Guinn Street. Most of the guys I grew up with are either on drugs, dead, or locked up.

It was God who gave me the hope, strength, and confidence to leave and follow my dreams.

It was God who taught me that life's greatest lesson is to trust in God.

And you know what? It all worked. I guess God gave me some really good advice.

**THE END**

# Acknowledgments

I'd like to thank Marvin Gaye, Richard Pryor, Miles Davis, Dr. Martin Luther King, Jr., Malcolm X, Marcus Garvey, Stevie Wonder, Luther Vandross, BB King, Atlantic Starr, Lakeside, Redd Foxx, Parliament-Funkadelic, George Clinton, Rick James, Michael Jackson, Prince, Eddie Murphy, Chris Rock, Duke Ellington, Charlie Parker, John Coltrane, Halle Berry, Lena Horne, Sharisse Scineaux, Dorothy Dandridge, Sammy Davis Jr., Sidney Poitier, Bill Cosby, Dick Gregory, Denzel Washington, Robin Harris, Ahmad Jamal, Al Green, Alexander O'Neal, Anita Baker, Barry White, The Isley Brothers, The Commodores, Curtis Mayfield, the guy who founded Popeye's Fried Chicken, Donna Summer, Earth Wind & Fire, En Vogue, The Gap Band, Heatwave, Vanessa Bell Calloway, Isaac Hayes, Janet Jackson, Spike Lee, Kool & the Gang, Maze featuring Frankie Beverly, Minnie Riperton, Jessie Lee Berry, James Baldwin, Richard Wright, Maya Angelou, Harriet Tubman, Muddy Waters, Howlin' Wolf, The O'Jays, Peabo Bryson, Roy Ayers, S.O.S Band, Smokie Norful, Lady Walker, Crystal McCrary Anthony, The Spinners, Marcus, Drak and Ryal (The Ill), Mr. Haley (my chemistry teacher who said I was going to end up in jail), The Stylistics, Teddy Pendergrass, Thelonius Monk, The Whispers, Run-DMC, Kurtis Blow, Grandmaster Flash and the Furious Five, LL Cool J, Rakim, Public Enemy, EPMD, KRS One, Common, Redman, Dr. Dre, Wu-Tang Clan, Ice Cube, Jay Z, Biggie, Nas, Outcast, UTFO, Guy, New Edition, Keith Sweat, Bobby Brown, Jody Watley, Don Cornelius, the entire cast of *Good Times* (especially John Amos), and my Lord and Savior Jesus Christ.

I've always said that I've lived my most of my life under the influence. I was under their influence.

I would like to give a very special thank you to Katherine Green, my career mentor and a woman who three times has changed my life for the better.

I want to thank my agent, Lane Zachary, and my publisher, Doug Seibold, for believing in me.

And finally, I want to thank my girlfriend, Rhadia Hursey. You were there when my ideas and dreams were just a bunch of ideas and dreams.

"A few what?"

"Hundred dollars. You'll make more if you work overtime."

I was thinking, *Hell, I'll work on Christmas, Easter, and New Year's for a hundred grand a year.* That was nearly triple what I was making in Baltimore. And I was only twenty-four years old!

I shook his hand. "Bill, you've got a deal."

We settled on a starting date three weeks from then.

I still had to tell Katherine. What would I say? She was very intimidating. The following Monday, I marched into her office. Then my knees started shaking and I started stuttering.

"Uh. K-K-Katherine?"

She must have known something was up, because she didn't even look up from her computer.

"I, uh, am taking this job at um, whew! WCBS and it's a really good opportun- (cough) I mean. Damn. Okay." I cleared my throat. "Well, you see, I, uh, prayed about it and oh well, God-told-me-this-is-what-I-should-do."

Katherine stopped typing, looked me in the eye, and said, "Well, God gave you some bad advice."